'Mohamed Mansour is an accomplished entrepreneur and a committed philanthropist who has been a valued partner to General Atlantic for over a decade. His leadership and dedication to the values of curiosity, integrity and innovation are closely aligned with our firm's core principles.'

Bill Ford, CEO, General Atlantic

'It was my honour and privilege to award an honorary doctorate to Dr Mansour in 2022 at our Spring Commencement, where he gave a truly uplifting speech to almost 20,000 people. His philanthropy, as well as the life-changing work being done by his non-profit for women in Egypt, is an inspiration to many people at NC State and we are immensely proud to call him one of our alumni.'

**Dr Randy Woodson, Chancellor,
North Carolina State University**

DRIVE
to
SUCCEED

The Making of an Egyptian Titan

MOHAMED MANSOUR

EBURY
PRESS

For my sons, Mansour and Loutfy, and my family

1

Published in 2023 by Ebury Press, an imprint of Ebury Publishing
20 Vauxhall Bridge Road,
London SW1V 2SA

Ebury Press is part of the Penguin Random House group of companies
whose addresses can be found at global.penguinrandomhouse.com

Text © Mohamed Mansour and Andrew Cave

Mohamed Mansour and Andrew Cave have asserted their right to be identified as the
authors of this work in accordance with the Copyright, Designs and Patents Act 1988

This edition first published by Ebury Press in 2023

www.penguin.co.uk

A CIP catalogue record for this book is available from the British Library

Hardback ISBN: 9781529911282

Typeset in 11.5/20pt Sabon Next LT Pro by Jouve (UK), Milton Keynes
Printed and bound in Great Britain by Clays Ltd, Elcograf S.p.A.

The authorised representative in the EEA is Penguin Random House Ireland,
Morrison Chambers, 32 Nassau Street, Dublin D02 YH68

Penguin Random House is committed to a sustainable future
for our business, our readers and our planet. This book is
made from Forest Stewardship® certified paper.

'Life is like riding a bicycle – to keep your balance you must keep moving'

Albert Einstein

CONTENTS

Foreword

**Tarek Adel, former Egyptian Ambassador
to the United Kingdom (2018–21)**

I knew the name Mohamed Mansour long before I knew the man. In Egypt, it is almost impossible not to know of his businesses – including his eponymous car companies, his Caterpillar distribution firm and other Mansour Group companies and investments.

As well as being one of the most important business leaders in Egypt of the last fifty years, he was also the government minister in charge of transport. During that period, he proved as adept at navigating public-sector bureaucracy and the corridors of political power as at handling international trade or high finance. His is a story of courage and inspiration, overcoming personal tragedy, political revolution and his family's fortune being confiscated not once but twice. It is also a story of how an entrepreneur created an Egyptian conglomerate that stretches across the globe.

I knew a little of his extraordinary personal story but was amazed at what I read in his candid, mesmerising story – the boyhood accident that nearly crippled him, the riches to rags to riches rollercoaster ride, and the success he achieved internationally, especially in Africa and the Middle East as well as in the USA and the United Kingdom.

I was appointed as the Egyptian Ambassador to the UK in 2018, and while I was in London we quickly became good friends. Mohamed is unfailingly warm, generous and, for someone so successful, surprisingly humble. His family means the world to him, but he also considers some of his most loyal colleagues and employees as extensions to his family. His wide-ranging philanthropic and charitable activities in Egypt and the UK are remarkable.

We share many interests ranging from football (I support Liverpool and he backs Manchester United) to the preservation of Egyptian antiquities. We also both have a deep affection for Egypt and the UK, and are keen to promote closer ties between the two countries.

When I became ambassador, relations between the nations were at a relatively low point. The suspension of direct flights between Britain and Sharm El Sheikh, imposed after a terrorist incident in 2015, had caused friction. Brexit was affecting the nature of our trade relationship with the UK and the European Union, as our bilateral trade relations were a part of the overall agreement that Egypt had with the European Union as a whole. The success we had in securing the lifting of the flights ban in

2019, and the signing of our bilateral trade agreement on the eve of the UK leaving the EU, were thanks to many factors. But the contribution of private sector leaders like Mohamed was important, particularly in terms of improving understanding of these issues.

So, what makes Mohamed Mansour stand out? First, his adaptability, whether it was being sent to school in the USA as a 15-year-old in the 1960s, later diversifying his business interests into different sectors and regions of the world, or navigating a political career as a government minister.

The second is his genius at problem-solving. He seeks counsel from trusted advisers, but has an instinct for knowing the right course and is able to be decisive and effective. Hence, his success as an entrepreneur and investor.

The third is his willingness to embrace change. How else to explain his success as an early investor in Facebook, Twitter and Spotify, or other disruptive businesses such as Uber and Airbnb? Traditional and conservative, yet modern and radical in other ways, Mohamed Mansour's fascinating and complex story is unique to him but inspiring to us all.

Preface

On a spring morning in Raleigh, North Carolina, I was driven to a music and sports venue, the 20,000-capacity PNC Arena, where I enjoyed one of the proudest moments of my whole life. This was the setting for North Carolina State University's 2022 graduation ceremony, known as 'the commencement'. I had been invited to deliver the keynote address to the graduating class of 2022, and to receive an honorary doctorate from my alma mater.

As I stood at the lectern and looked out at the thousands of graduates in their crimson gowns, I could not help but reflect on how much my life had changed since I had been in the graduating class myself in the spring of 1968.

Back then, a doctor had warned me that I may have cancer. Within four months of my graduation, the diagnosis was confirmed; a surgeon had to remove my left kidney, after finding a malignant tumour the size of a teacup.

Since then, I have always pushed that trauma to the back of my mind, rarely thinking or talking about it. Until now.

It was the biggest challenge of my life, but even then, aged 20, it was not the first time I had diced with death or had to overcome adversity. I had been confined to bed for three years from the age of ten after being run over in a terrible car accident. Things went bad in a different way when I was 18 and our family's business and other assets were confiscated by Egypt's socialist government; my father went from being extremely wealthy to struggling on a low government worker's wage, and my allowance as a student dried up. To stay at university, just to feed myself and pay off my debts, I had to work as a waiter in a diner in Raleigh to support myself.

• • •

In the 54 years between those contrasting graduation ceremonies of 1968 and 2022, I have pursued a varied business career, built a family, served in government and created, what I hope is, a positive legacy. The fortitude, good luck and perseverance I experienced in adversity is what ultimately motivated me to develop this book in collaboration with the author and journalist Andrew Cave. I am a private man, not always comfortable talking about myself, but I am proud of what I have achieved, individually and in collaboration with my family and friends over the last half century. It brings me joy to share my memories.

Alongside my siblings, I have created some of the largest businesses in North Africa and the Middle East that employ tens of thousands of people, mostly in the developing world. *Forbes* magazine described us as the number one family business in the Arab world. We have partnered with some of the greatest global brands from General Motors to Caterpillar and McDonald's. We have invested in dozens of technology companies, including Airbnb, Uber, Facebook, Twitter and Spotify, and by doing so I like to think we have played a small part in financing some of the technology that has shaped both today's and tomorrow's worlds.

A three-year period as Egypt's minister of transport was the hardest job of my life but a huge honour. I am especially proud of the Lead Foundation, a non-profit that I established in Egypt 20 years ago. It has provided financial support to hundreds of thousands of women-owned small businesses in North Africa with more than 4 million loans since it was set up.

Perhaps all those organisations would still have been set up – all those opportunities for other people would still have been created – had I lost my leg in that car accident in 1958, or flunked my course in 1966, or been severely debilitated by cancer from 1968 onwards.

Others have dropped out of university, or overcome health scares and setbacks, and gone on to great things. But the chips fell fortuitously for me. I learned never to allow adversity to triumph. Decades later, standing in the PNC Arena where Bruce Springsteen and Beyoncé had belted out their songs to a similarly large capacity crowd, I was almost embarrassed to be there. I felt humbled but also so very lucky.

Sometimes we all need luck. And I have spent my adult life working as hard as I can to capitalise on the good fortune, luck and opportunities that I have been given.

Never taking anything for granted. Never assuming success will continue. And never allowing a setback to define me.

Mohamed Mansour, July 2023

CHAPTER ONE

Three years of solitude

My life very nearly ended when I was just ten years old. It was Revolution Day, 23 July 1958, commemorating the uprising in Egypt six years earlier that had led to the toppling of King Farouk and ushered in a wave of revolutionary politics in the Arab world. Everywhere there were celebrations, but my world ground to a halt that day.

I had been spending the day at our family villa in the Mediterranean city of Alexandria. My father had earlier gone to Cairo, and I had accompanied him to the airport. As our driver returned me home, my eldest brother, Ismail, who was just 14, took the keys to one of my father's cars. Two of my cousins jumped in with him and they drove around the block, showing off to two German girls in the building next door to ours.

The teenaged Ismail tended to live life on the edge. My mother, tipped off by our driver, headed out onto the balcony to see what was going on and started to scream at Ismail to stop. I rushed out to warn my brother, but Ismail did not see my small frame as I ran into the road. 'Stop! Stop before you get to the door where she will see you!' I cried, but instead of applying the brakes, he pressed the accelerator. I can still hear the roar of the engine, followed by a loud screeching sound and then a crunch and excruciating pain as I was crushed against the 5-metre-high iron gates of our home. The car's tall 1950s bumper propelled me into the ground and my leg became jammed. When I tried to stand, there was blood everywhere and almost no leg beneath me.

One of my cousins rushed me to Alexandria's Mowassa hospital in my father's Pontiac. I remember a chaotic scene with doctors and nurses running around. Medical care in those days was not what it is today. My only other time in hospital until then was when my appendix was removed when I was six. This time the atmosphere was one of panic and fear. My father returned home to find his son hospitalised and fighting for his life.

The doctors did not seem optimistic and although I was almost delirious, I recall hushed conversations about whether I would lose a limb or may not even survive. My temperature rose at night. I had a dangerously high fever and that then dropped in the morning, day after day. One doctor told me he would have to amputate my leg because there was almost no bone there and the infection was spreading to the rest of my body. I was on the verge of going into a coma.

I remember pleading with my father not to let me lose my leg: 'Please, Dad. No. No. No.' I was a keen sports player, a fast runner and the top swimmer in my class at school. I had won a cabinet of medals. Ismail and Youssef, my other elder brother, were also very competitive but I was known for being an adventurous, athletic boy who was always running and playing. I could not imagine being without a limb and refused to allow my leg to be lost but the head doctor disagreed. As my fever raged at night, he told my parents I would only survive if my infected leg was removed. 'Dad, please,' I cried. 'I will be fine. I cannot lose my leg.' My mother sat with me through the night, at the end of my bed, distraught and in tears.

I was next moved to another ward and put into isolation to stop the infection spreading and the fever slowly started to recede. However, what really saved my leg and probably my life was the intervention of Gawad Hamada, a doctor who had seen me collecting trophies for athletics at my school. Orthopaedic surgeons, as I was to learn, bluntly tell it like it is, but Dr Hamada told his colleagues that they had to save my leg as he could not bear to see me handicapped for the rest of my life. Instead, he removed the blood-stained plaster cast on my leg and performed an operation on my foot. The infection alarmingly increased because blood was seeping out day after day. Another doctor suggested wrapping my frail damaged limb in silver foil. Miraculously, this managed to stem the infection, and I was dosed with strong antibiotics.

Amazingly, my leg was saved. But I still had to remain in

hospital for three months. Dr Hamada had been my absolute saviour, a miracle doctor. He had been strong when others were fearful and weak. An extremely serious man who possessed all the gravitas that his role required. I never saw him smile. But he did save my leg, and my life, and I am forever indebted to him. Three years later, I went to London to be examined by a well-known orthopaedic surgeon called Sir Reginald Watson-Jones who was also deeply impressed. When he examined the original X-rays and saw I was still able to walk, he said that no one could have done any better. But my recuperation came with a heavy price as, even after I was discharged, I was confined to my bed for most of the next three years.

Hour after hour, day after day, I lay in bed. Barred from moving or being moved, I would sleep sitting up in my room. The cast was so heavy that a pillow was put behind my back and my arm tucked under my chin. That is how I would doze off, but it was not comfortable.

I was confined to a large bedroom with a high ceiling which I shared with my brothers Ismail and Youssef. We would sit up in bed, chatting to each other and sharing the events of the day. Sometimes, when my father and mother were not around, my brothers and I got up during the night and played. But mostly I was alone as my brothers went outside to play with our cousins. At first, there was no television so all I had were my Batman, Superman and Lone Ranger comic books, which I would read endlessly. Later, my parents bought me a small, black-and-white television set. I was desperately in need of distraction. And the pain in my leg could be excruciating. All I ever wished was for it to stop and for me to be able to run, or even just to walk.

Those things I had taken for granted as a small boy were over. No more kicking a ball around with my friends at school; no more games of racquetball with my brothers; no more playing on Nefertiti and Aida beaches at Alexandria in the Montaza Palace, the royal residence and gardens so beloved by kings Fuad and Farouk; no more imagining I was T.E. Lawrence as I galloped on horseback over sand dunes in the desert beyond Cairo.

And no more Christmases at the Old Cataract Hotel at Aswan in the Nubian Desert, the legendary property built in 1899 by the British tourism pioneer Thomas Cook and immortalised in *Death on the Nile*, which Agatha Christie wrote during a year-long stay there in the 1930s. In the middle of December 1958, my family departed for their vacation at the Old Cataract, leaving me in bed with only our staff for company over the next three weeks. I imagined the journey they would take: the thrilling train journey south from Alexandria to Upper Egypt; the horse-drawn carriages that would be waiting for them at the end of the line to carry them to the hotel; seeing the horses and the donkeys in their stables; the guest rooms with their high ceilings, whirring fans, mosquito nets and verandas overlooking the Nile, where feluccas sailed gently by; the projector room where they would watch Hollywood and Egyptian movies; and the glamour and elegance of the ballroom. After missing out on another family Christmas, my father on his return to Alexandria told me he had bought me some land close to the Old Cataract Hotel. For him it may have been more than just a gift, perhaps it was also atonement.

I felt abandoned – not only during the Christmas break, but throughout the year, especially during the summer when I would be left at home while my parents and siblings visited the beach. My friends would turn up occasionally, but for day after day, I lay alone in my room with only my thoughts for company. I learned to be resilient and self-sufficient. I was in pain, physically and mentally, but I didn't want to show any emotion or weakness. It was a terrible thing to go through, but it was character building. I matured quickly for my age. I became a thinker and found that I was happy in my own company.

The highlight of my day would come in the evenings, when my father would visit me after work and we would listen together to the BBC World Service and Voice of America on my father's Zenith radio, one of his proudest possessions. Egypt was isolated from the rest of the world, and while President Nasser may have had some justification in nationalising the Suez Canal, the conflict had the undesired effect of driving the nation into the arms of the Soviet Union, one of the worst things to happen to our country in modern times.

Many young Egyptians studied in Soviet universities and military schools, including the future president, Hosni Mubarak, who trained as a military pilot in Kyrgyzstan. Soviet leader Nikita Khrushchev visited Egypt in the early 1960s to confer the communist country's highest honour, the star of the Hero of the Soviet

Union and the Order of Lenin, on Nasser. My sister Rawya was often one of the Egyptian children invited to greet arriving heads of state and other dignitaries with flowers at the airport in Alexandria; on one such occasion, she handed a bouquet to Khrushchev. Little could she have known, as she innocently smiled at the First Secretary of the Communist Party, that here was the man who approved the building of the Berlin Wall, brutally crushed a revolt in Hungary and brought the world to the brink of nuclear catastrophe during the Cuban missile crisis.

The misery that we felt as a country over the alliance with the Soviet Union matched my own. Egypt was isolated and closed off from the non-Soviet world. I, too, was trapped and yearning for freedom. My father would sometimes play Arabic music such as the Egyptian singer Om Kalthoum, who was known as the Star of the Middle East. He would talk to me about business and what he did during the day. I listened intently, absorbing all he told me like a sponge.

For a very long time, I was not able to get any fresh air; my days were spent sitting in a room, mostly by myself. I could not go to the open-air cinema or meet my friends. I had been lined up to be a prefect and probably head boy. When school restarted that autumn, some friends visited but I still felt like a forgotten person, with everyone getting on with their lives without me. *What could I do? How could I stay calm? What was I to do to occupy my time?* I thought a great deal about this and decided to make a day-by-day plan. I started to read and studied fervently as these were the only things that I could do.

Gradually, my lot improved. But it was very slow progress. It was agony when they replaced my cast, which at that time reached to the top of my leg. After about a year, I was strong enough to be carried from my room throughout the rest of the house. I would lie relatively flat in our station wagon and look out of the car window. It felt like I was able to breathe again. Our gardener made me a kite and I discovered that I loved to watch it soar, so free.

I could visit the beach again but would have to lie on a chair with my leg propped up. However, breathing in sea air and seeing the Mediterranean again meant so much. It was there that I met one of the most famous performing artists and actors of the 1950s in the Middle East on several occasions, Abdel Halim Hafez, who had been touched by my story and contacted my parents about a meeting. He had previously overcome adversity himself, after contracting a rare disease as a boy that was gradually damaging his liver (and would eventually cause his premature death, aged 47, in 1977). Then, he was about 30 years old and would join us on the beach for hours at a time; I loved to sit and talk with him. He even filmed a scene for one of his movies by our beach cabin, performing a song called 'In a Day, a Month, a Year'. He was our Elvis – an Egyptian superstar – and I was greatly saddened when I heard of his passing.

I felt that I was in heaven when I was able to sit in our garden again. I would take my lunch in the garden and my father and mother would join me, while my brothers played football or games like hide-and-seek. My mother was passionate about her garden, which regularly won awards for being the best in the city.

She cultivated a unique violet-coloured tulip: the only one of its kind in Egypt. Its flowers were often the highlight of the Greek-styled garden festivals in the city. That would be enough to give me hope for another three or four months, as I continued to battle pain and struggle with the lack of mobility. I would sit in our garden and listen to the birdsong.

Very slowly I learned to stand, and to walk again. I had to build strength again in my legs and arms. I used crutches for a very long time, and then the cast that had reached the top of my leg was replaced with one that ran from my heel to my knee. Eventually, after having surgery in London to fix a metal pin to the broken bones, I walked with a cane and a custom-made leather boot, which I would continue to wear until 1964, by which time I was studying in America.

CHAPTER TWO

Roots and revolutions

I was born into an old Egyptian family in January 1948 and grew up as the third of five children to my father, Loutfy Mansour, and mother, Nazly Akef Fouad.

Our family's roots went deep into the soil of the Middle East. Our ancestors were thought to have migrated to the Nile Delta from what was to become Saudi Arabia in the Middle Ages. Over centuries, the family acquired land around Alexandria. My father came from a line of cotton entrepreneurs. My paternal grandfather, Amin Bek Mansour, worked with King Fuad I in the 1920s and was in charge of one of the king's palaces. ('Bek' was a title rather like 'Sir' in the UK today.)

My mother grew up in Cairo and her family had important connections in Ottoman Turkey and throughout the Levant by marriage. At one time a family member provided financial assistance to Kemal Atatürk during his creation of the modern, secular Turkish state. Her father, Akef Bek Fouad, was an Ottoman governor-representative in Lebanon; her uncle, an ambassador who was married to a cousin of King Farouk.

My mother was a neighbour of my father's uncle, whom my father would visit often. She would look out and see this young man coming to visit his uncle. To attract his attention, on one occasion she dropped a handkerchief from her window. He looked up and saw a petite girl with dark hair and blue eyes. She was elegant and striking; people would later compare her to the Hollywood actress Elizabeth Taylor.

Gradually, as my father kept appearing, she would open her window so they could talk. The families finally agreed to a chaperoned meeting, with the purpose that they would eventually marry. That is how things were done in those days. My father proposed a few weeks later and they got married in 1939, just as war was breaking out in Europe and refugees from France, Italy and Greece were flooding into the country.

It was a deliriously happy time for them, even as the world was falling apart. When the decisive second battle of El Alamein took place between the Axis German and Italian forces, commanded by Erwin Rommel, and an Allied force led by Field Marshal Bernard Montgomery, in 1942, my parents were living in what was still a British protectorate and could hear the distant sound of guns. Victoria College, the British school where my parents sent my brothers and me, became a naval and military hospital for Allied servicemen and women, with the school moved temporarily to the San Stefano hotel.

My parents' first child, a boy, died during childbirth in 1939. Four years later in Cairo, my mother gave birth to Ismail. In the spring of 1945, my mother, then seven months pregnant with Youssef, travelled to the rural governate of El Sharkia, to the north-east of Cairo, to support her sister who was due to give birth to a boy, who would be called Ahmed El Maghraby. When my aunt went into labour in the hospital, it seemed to trigger something with my mother, who prematurely gave birth to Youssef a few days later.

Three years later, in 1948, my heavily pregnant mother was visiting her sister Dawlat in El Sharkia when she gave birth to me. My father was away on business in the USA at the time. As he had done before Ismail and Youssef were born, he opened the Quran at a random page and looked for the name of a prophet. The text opened at the story of Younes (or Jonah in the Jewish and Christian tradition, a Hebrew prophet known for an encounter with a whale), and concluded that if the baby was male, it would take that prophet's name. But when my mother's sister called my father and had given the happy news, 'Younes has been born', the timing prompted a change of heart. By chance, I had been born on Mawlid al-Nabi, the public holiday in Egypt and much of the Arab world that marks the birth date of the Prophet Muhammed. I was named Mohamed Younes Loutfy Mansour.

We lived in Cairo until 1952, spending the first four years in an apartment, when my father left his public sector job in Cairo to form Loutfy Mansour and Sons. As the cotton trade was based around Alexandria, the family relocated to the Mediterranean coast. In 1954 my mother bought a villa, which was renovated to a very high standard. That year, my sister Rawya was born. By 1956, the villa was ready for us to move into. It would be my home for the rest of my childhood, and the site of my car accident in 1958. My other sibling, Yasseen, was born in 1961, by which time I was 13, and recovering from the accident.

My mother was a beautiful, calm lady who devoted her life to raising her family. I rarely, if ever, heard her shout, lose her temper, or say a derogatory word. I did not always find it easy to talk to my father so I would confide in her and she would bring up the matter I was concerned about with him. She never went to university but was quick and bright, equipped with cultured taste and a talent for design expressed in the furnishing of a beautiful antiques and flower-filled Italianate villa built in suburban Gianaclis in the 1910s. It is still featured in a book of noted palaces of Egypt today. Whenever she had the time, she would be on the lookout for antiques, carpets and beautiful paintings.

She was the best negotiator I have ever known. She would ask the price of something and when they would quote her E£100, she would offer E£5. I used to be horrified, telling her the shopowner would think we were showing no respect and would kick us out, but she would end up shaking hands at E£20. She was more careful with money than my father, who she thought could be too generous. Sometimes we thought she took this a little far; when we were older, my brothers and I would slip the staff at her house something extra because she would seldom give them a raise. When she came to see us in the USA, she even tried to negotiate in JCPenney, the department store, just like she did in Alexandria!

She was my father's closest adviser, in both business and home matters, where he taught us to be ambitious and to improve ourselves. Ismail was confident, charismatic and kind. If he ever saw somebody in need, he would want to help them. Tall and good-looking, he was also the naughtiest, frequently getting into fights and breaking our family's strict rules. He was physically strong, athletic and had a loyal group of friends. But the car accident affected him badly. Some cruel people said he was a bad person who wanted to hurt his own brother, which was wrong. The accident was as much my fault because I ran out in front of the car, but everyone was sympathetic rather than condemning due to the injury. This constant chatter upset Ismail and he grew angry about it. I was everything to him; the only one of the three brothers at the time who he listened to, and the accident served to unbalance a lot of things for him.

Youssef was the exact opposite of Ismail: very calm, serious and studious; essentially more cautious than his brother. He was always there for me as a child, and we were extremely close. Compared to my two older brothers' contrasting personalities of reckless and risk-averse, I was somewhere in the middle.

My sister Rawya saw me as her protector, even though she was generally over-protected by the entire family. I once hit a friend who insulted her. As a child I would joke that I was going to be 'the hero of the world' – she would reply that she would be the mightiest!

I think Yasseen, who is 13 years my junior, regarded me as something of a father figure, particularly after our father died when he was 15. Yasseen is a workaholic; like the famous Criollo horse of the Argentinian Pampas, with a reputation for long-distance endurance, never giving up and honouring whatever you commit to – all things that I learned from our father. I have long regarded him as my rock; hard-working, brilliant, kind and a fighter. He is very bright, very good with numbers, and is a lot of fun to be around. We still speak almost every day. We bring out the best in each other. He likes to do everything himself, whereas I like to delegate.

My elder brothers and I stood out at Victoria College, and not only because Ismail was such a big and strong young man. As Egyptians, we were in the minority. The private boys' school we attended together was founded by a group of British businessmen in 1902. It was originally conceived by the British community in the city as the British School of Egypt, but its planned opening was delayed as a result of a cholera outbreak, and by the time its inaugural enrolment of 26 boys took their places for class, Queen Victoria had died and the founders had changed its name in homage to the late empress-queen.

Although established by the British expatriate community in the city, Victoria College was open to all. Its alumni, known as 'Old Victorians', would go on to include royalty such as King Hussain of Jordan; the renowned Palestinian intellectual Edward

Said; the Saudi arms dealer Adnan Khashoggi; and Hollywood actor Omar Sharif. But over half its students were British-born, and it became a symbol of British hegemony in the region for half a century. When the school was founded at the dawn of the twentieth century, Egypt was still technically an Ottoman province governed by the sultan's representative. However, the British had occupied Egypt since the 1880s, after which the country's effective ruler had been the British consul-general, the Earl of Cromer, Sir Evelyn Baring, a colonial archetype known by some of his contemporaries as 'Over-Baring'. Cromer, who 'ruled' Egypt until 1907, lived up to the stereotype when he was rudely dismissive of the quality of the education provided elsewhere in the country by 'native' schools during a speech at Victoria in 1906.

Cromer gave his name to one of the school houses that students were organised into. Some of the other houses had similar colonial connotations, including 'Kitchener'. The school would go on to be regarded as arguably the Arab world's most prestigious academic institution. The education was secular and liberal by the standards of the time, but its rules and regulations, codified in the student handbook that we were all given, were enforced rigidly. By cane, if necessary. The first rule was 'English is the language of the school'.

School traditions and events were central highlights of the calendar – sports days in May, prize-giving days on the eve of the summer break, school productions in December. The annual Victoria College Speech Day became a national news event, where political leaders would deliver de facto state-of-the-nation addresses.

School hours were 8am–5pm Monday through Friday, with short breaks. Saturday was a half-day and Sundays were free. The school year was divided into three three-month terms: Michaelmas, Easter and Summer. Classes ended in the middle of December for a three-week break over Christmas. The teachers were British, the lessons were taught in English, and the students practised cricket, tennis and football (although, strangely, not rugby, the other sporting staple of the English private school). I was no better than an average student and liked to joke around in class, but I was an avid runner, swimmer and footballer, and loved learning about history, my favourite subject.

I started going to Victoria as a five-year-old kindergarten student. It was 1953, the year of Queen Elizabeth II's coronation, a year after the military coup that toppled King Farouk. Egypt was in the throes of decolonisation, with 'Inglizi out!' a popular nationalist refrain. When I joined kindergarten, the school had around seven hundred students comprising nearly thirty nationalities; although still dominated by children of British expats, the school was living up to its Latin motto of *cuncti gens una sumus* ('we are one people').

It consistently adhered to a secular programme, although some students, including my future father-in-law, Mansour Hassan, had campaigned unsuccessfully for Islam to become a more prominent feature of the curriculum. Following the Suez Crisis in 1956, when I was in the first grade, the school's connection to Britain was formerly removed. The British teachers were deported, and the school was renamed Victory College. The universally accepted story is that the school went into gradual decline. But the new teachers, many of them Egyptians and Greeks, seemed far less strict and we had more fun. I am sure I was still receiving a world-class education, and the old boys' network remained influential, even if the Old Victorians of its heyday are dwindling in number today.

My brothers and I were 'day boys'. Every morning I'd take the 15-minute journey on the tram from our home in San Stefano, only a few hundred metres from the sea, close enough to breathe in the salty air as I walked, schoolbag in hand, to the station. I'd pay my fare to the immaculately-dressed tram conductor, talk to other boys on the tram who were heading to Victoria or gaze out of the window as we passed through the coastal suburb of Ramleh. I would watch cars passing along the Corniche, the promenade designed in the 1870s by the Italian-Egyptian architect Pietro Avoscani that hugs the Mediterranean.

I loved Alexandria, the city of legend – Alexander the Great's capital city where Euclid discovered geometry, Aristarchus deduced that the Earth rotated on an axis that revolved around the Sun and Cleopatra studied in the Great Library. The city flourished in the nineteenth century as the hub of Egypt's commerce, especially the cotton trade, drew a cosmopolitan mix of Greeks, Italians, French, Jews and Levantine Arabs to its walls. But things had changed by the time of the Suez Crisis of 1956. Victoria College's teachers were not the only foreigners expelled from Alexandria, and the city's cultural grandeur began to crumble.

Nevertheless, to Egyptians, Alexandria remained the 'Pearl of the Mediterranean. The Greek, Italian and French quarters sparkled with vitality, colour and excitement, while ancient churches and temples were a mosaic of history and faith. As boys we would visit the Montaza Palace, a summer mansion overlooking the Mediterranean that would be used by future presidents Nasser, Sadat and Mubarak. Close to our home was the glamorous San Stefano Hotel, where businessmen and tourists sipped Martinis, smoked aromatic cigarettes and gazed out at the Eastern Harbour. The hotel had an amazing open-air cinema, which showed the latest movies from Hollywood as we sat under the bright stars. My friends and I would watch the films and swap the cards we collected of movie stars like Liz Taylor and James Dean.

• • •

My father was a strong, charismatic and intelligent man who showed great perseverance and was highly principled. He was religious, reading the Quran more than 600 times. He would study it every day and spend hours praying, even during his many travels for work. One of my most treasured possessions is a handwritten Arabic script dated April 1975 that was found inside the pages of my father's Quran, pledging to serve his family and Egypt, do good through his cotton company and help the poor. I keep it framed on the desk in my office.

One downside of his care was that it could be overpowering. We went to the mosque on Fridays when I was not allowed to go to my youth club. During holidays, we had to be with the family. At times, he would come across as too strict, but this was typical of his generation. We could be naughty as kids. We made an agreement with the chauffeur that he would toot the car horn whenever he was bringing our father home, so we could get ready to stand in military-style salute. Ambitious and hard-working, he was among the first Egyptian students to attend Cambridge University, where he studied agriculture at St John's College from 1929–32. I later visited the college and found that he had been somewhat exaggerating when he told me that he was a top student, but he did graduate.

On his return to Egypt, he worked as an under-secretary in the Ministry of Agriculture, which is where he was working when I was born in 1948. It was the time of the first Arab–Israeli war following the Israeli Declaration of Independence. He went on to leave public service after a disagreement with the ministry over agricultural policy. He got a job in the private sector, working with a man called Robert Khouri, who ran a major cotton-exporting company, agreeing a percentage of sales. The company's big break came in 1950. The US Army, engaged in the Korean War, needed cotton for parachutes and Mr Khouri was able to seal a major export deal.

My father soon began to excel at business, carving out a reputation as a fine salesman. He travelled all over the world, fitting in seamlessly with whatever culture he was in at the time. He was regarded as Egyptian in Egypt, American in America and English in the UK. In 1952, he set up his own business, Loutfy Mansour and Sons, becoming one of the first Egyptians to own and run their own cotton-trading company. He exported Egyptian long staple cotton, the best in the world, from Alexandria. He already had relationships with spinning and weaving firms in the UK and California, as well as in the Soviet Union and China. Within only a few years he had overtaken his great friend Mr Khouri's operation and became Egypt's largest privately owned cotton exporter.

All this was of enormous consequence to our family. Cotton was Egypt's main industry at a time of economic growth. Alexandria's stock exchange was the fifth most active stock market in the world. The Egyptian pound was stronger than the US dollar. The cotton trade was very profitable, which made our family wealthy. My father bought out some partners who had helped him start the business between 1952 and 1954. By 1956 the company was second, by size, only to the cotton assets owned by the government in Egypt. Loutfy Mansour and Sons employed 70 people and made a handsome net profit of around E£300,000 per year.

My father had to keep his ear to the ground to know how the political and economic environment affected his buyers in the US, Europe and the Soviet Union. Geopolitics and macroeconomics were of great interest to him.

• • •

I loved being raised in Alexandria and was fascinated and inspired by its history and its people. It had been a centre of Hellenic scholarship and science. An ancient lighthouse was one of the Seven Wonders of the Ancient World. Its storied library was reincarnated in the disc-shaped ultra-modern Bibliotheca Alexandrina. The city still has Greco-Roman landmarks, old-world cafés and sandy beaches while its fifteenth-century seafront Qaitbay Citadel is a museum. Although it later went into decline, it was a beautiful vibrant city in the 1950s, as the wealth from the cotton industry supported education and healthcare. We lived very comfortably, with around twenty staff, including nannies, housekeepers, cooks, chauffeurs and gardeners.

My mother's family came from noble descent. My brothers and I were brought up on stories of my mother's grandfather, who had lived an extraordinary life for nearly a hundred years. He was born Fuad Pasha Tugay in Cairo in 1835, the son of an army general, Hassan Pasha, an inspector of Sudan. ('Pasha' was an Ottoman title equivalent to the British title of 'lord' or 'viceroy'.) He graduated from the Cairo Military Academy and was promoted to the rank of admiral in the Egyptian army. One story recounted a moment where the two military men stood to attention at a parade. When Hassan Pasha saluted, his son said, 'Dad, you don't have to salute me!' To which Hassan Pasha responded, 'I am not saluting you, you idiot, I'm saluting the uniform!'

Fuad Pasha moved to Istanbul, Turkey, in 1869 and after helping to suppress tribal uprisings in Kirkuk in modern-day Iraq, he was promoted to *murliva* (brigadier-general). He served in the Russo–Turkish war in the 1870s, becoming a national hero after the successful battle of Elena. He acquired the nickname 'Deli', reflecting the Turkish word for 'mad' or 'crazy', an affectionate reference to his fearlessness as a military leader. For the remainder of his life, he was known as Deli Fuad Pasha. I always imagined that Ismail had inherited that 'crazy' gene from our great-grandfather.

Following the Russo–Turkish war, the hero of Elena was appointed the sultan's counsel or *aide-de-camp*. But he became disillusioned with the slow pace of modernisation and reform in the faltering and fracturing empire. One of my favourite stories about him involved the sultan pulling a gun on him after he had stormed into the ruler's office without permission. Deli Fuad Pasha opened his vest and urged the sultan to 'shoot!' Happily, no shots were fired that day. But his liberal views led him to be exiled to Damascus, Syria, by Abdulhamid II, the last sultan to exert absolute power over an empire that had survived for more than 600 years. He returned to Istanbul in 1908 after the Young Turk Revolution, which ended with Abdulhamid II dethroned and a parliamentary system restored. What remained of the monarchy's power passed to Abdulhamid's half-brother, who became Sultan Mehmed V. In 1909, Deli Fuad Pasha was appointed to the Ottoman Empire's senate, the *Meclis-i Ayan*. During the Balkan Wars, he took part in the defence of Istanbul, before retiring from the military, aged 78, in 1913.

The empire's misjudged alliance with Germany and the other central powers during World War I precipitated its final collapse. The last sultan was crowned Mehmed VI in the summer of 1918. At the end of World War I, the British and its Allies prepared for the partition of Ottoman territory by occupying Istanbul and other provincial cities. In 1919, shortly after the outbreak of the Turkish War of Independence, a field marshal who had emerged as a leader of nationalist resistance, Mustafa Kemal Atatürk, called an assembly at Sivas, a city in central Turkey, to agree the foundational principles and policies of the independence movement. Deli Fuad Pasha backed the pro-independence movement *Kuva-yi*

Milliye and played a key role in the fall of the government of Damat Ferit Pasha in 1920 by ensuring that the decisions of the Sivas Congress were accepted by Mehmed VI. Another of the last sultan's ministers and advisers was the former newspaper editor Ali Kemal, great-grandfather to another journalist-turned-politician, the former British prime minister Boris Johnson.

The war of independence ultimately led to the abolition of the sultanate and the creation of the modern republic of Turkey, headed by Atatürk, in 1922. The same year, Ali Kemal, who had backed the British occupiers who wanted to keep the sultan on the throne, was killed by a paramilitary group. By this time, Deli Fuad Pasha was approaching 90. He died in Istanbul in 1931 and was interred in the city's great Eyup Sultan mosque.

Despite this historic hinterland, my own family has always been low-key. My father was committed to helping the poor and was always respectful of a person's humanity, whatever their background. He would greet a labourer in the same way as he would a government minister. He taught us to respect everyone. He was the ultimate role model for me.

Egypt was highly unstable in the late 1950s and early 1960s, which created difficulties for my father. Three years after World War II, Egypt was at war with Israel. In 1952, when I was four, a group of officers led by Gamal Abdel Nasser, including Anwar Sadat, sought to oust the British and overthrow King Farouk, eventually succeeding in declaring Egypt a republic a year later. In 1954, Nasser was named Egypt's prime minister.

In January 1956, Nasser announced a constitution under

which Egypt became a socialist Arab state with a one-party political system and Islam as the official religion. In June, 99.9% of the 5 million Egyptians voting marked their ballots for Nasser, the only candidate, for president. The constitution was approved by 99.8%.

Nasser wanted to build a high dam south of Aswan to generate electricity for the nation and protect the area from flooding. The Mediterranean Sea around Egypt would turn brown in August, due to the mud and silt that would be swept up from modern-day Ethiopia and Lake Victoria.

A secret arms contract had been signed with Czechoslovakia, part of the communist bloc. The UK and USA had agreed to put up $270 million to finance the first stage of the Aswān High Dam project. But in July 1956, the US Secretary of State John Dulles cancelled the offer; the next day Britain followed suit. Egypt applied to the World Bank for $300 million of international finance to build the dam. When the World Bank also declined to provide the funds, President Nasser responded by announcing in Alexandria that the government would nationalise the Suez Canal Company to collect the tolls that the president estimated would pay for the dam within a few years. The company, which had been given a long lease for the canal, was owned primarily by British and French shareholders. In October and November 1956, Israel, Britain and France declared war. Israeli forces invaded Egyptian Sinai and British and French paratroopers landed along the Suez Canal.

I was eight years old when these momentous events were happening. I recall waiting for my school bus to pick me up, when I heard sirens and looked up to see warplanes flying overhead.

The RAF strafed the airport at Alexandria. On another occasion I remember my mother coming out when I was playing with my brothers, screaming at us to come back inside the house. Air-raid sirens would ring out at night and our windows were covered by dark-blue paper to block out any lights. We would hide under our beds.

Egyptian forces responded by blocking the canal to all shipping by sinking 40 ships. The three allies had attained a few of their military objectives, but the canal was useless and remained closed until March 1957. Heavy political pressure from the USA and the USSR led to a withdrawal. President Eisenhower had strongly warned the UK not to invade and threatened damage to the British financial system by selling the US government's sterling bonds.

As a result of the conflict, the British prime minister Anthony Eden resigned; Canadian external affairs minister Hester Pearson won the Nobel Peace Prize; and the Soviets may have been emboldened to invade Hungary. Historians have concluded that the crisis and withdrawal symbolised the end of Britain's status as one of the world's major powers.

The Egyptian media was very jingoistic and the feeling in the country was very much that Egypt had won the war. It was certainly a great political victory for Mr Nasser, but it also heralded the Soviet era in my homeland, with the USSR agreeing to help fund the high dam and the influence of the Soviet bloc permeating deeply into Egypt and the Middle East.

• • •

My father continued to focus on his business during this tumul-
tuous period during the late 1950s and early 1960s. He could be
stern; not the kind of father that you had a nickname for but one
who we would simply call 'Daddy'. We were very respectful. When
he walked into our room, I would sit up while Ismail and Youssef
stood to attention like soldiers. With my mother, we would kiss
her hand. We were taught always to exhibit perfect manners. My
father was a little more lenient with me than with my siblings,
which meant that I was able to argue with him a little, in a way
that my brothers were not allowed; I would suggest things and he
would sit and explain to me what was possible and how the world
worked. A family friend Simone Khouri, whom I called Aunt
Simone, visited me and prayed fervently for my recovery. She
pledged to walk the 20km from Versailles to Paris giving money
to every church on the way if I recovered – a promise she honoured in 1960 when I was able to walk a little with crutches.

My father dealt in cotton exports in commodity markets all
over the world. He would speak on the phone to mills and negotiate the future delivery of crops. He would give his own price and
make a deal. If the price of a commodity that was currently in the
fields and had not been collected turned out to be higher than his
price, he would still honour the original bargain.

He owned a lot of mills and land and accumulated great
wealth. But everything changed for my father when he decided to
go into politics and enter the Egyptian parliament. Nasser was an
autocratic dictator who disliked businesspeople and exercised his
socialist desire to redistribute private wealth. My father was an

obvious target. The president began nationalising strategic indus-tries and in 1963 amalgamated Egypt's 58 cotton companies into 4, making my father chairman and chief executive of the largest one, Port Said Cotton Company.

After a year, my father arrived at his office to find a man in military uniform telling him he was taking charge of the Port Said Company. My father was ousted, and a process was begun to sequestrate his properties and land. Virtually everything my father owned was confiscated. From then on, he worked for the state and received $75 a month. He was a good man and a patriot and had not invested a single cent outside of Egypt. Yet, with one decree, everything was taken. He was ordered to stay at home. He was denounced as a capitalist and imperialist who had contributed to the ruin of the nation and various spurious charges were laid against him. Essentially, he was under house arrest. This was Egyptian-style communism, and it triggered revolutionary conse-quences for Libya, Sudan, Syria, Algeria and very nearly for Jordan.

Nasser's popularity in Egypt and the Arab world skyrocketed after he nationalised the Suez Canal Company and won a political victory in the subsequent Suez Crisis. Calls for Pan-Arab unity under his leadership increased, culminating with the formation of the United Arab Republic with Syria in 1958–61. In 1962, Nasser began a series of major socialist measures and modernisation reforms in Egypt. He began his second presidential term in March 1965 after his political opponents were banned from running. Fol-lowing Egypt's defeat by Israel in the Six-Day War of 1967, Nasser resigned, but he returned to office after popular demonstrations called for his reinstatement. By 1968, Nasser had appointed himself prime minister, launched the War of Attrition to regain the Israeli-occupied Sinai Peninsula, and begun a process of depoliticising the military. He remains an important figure in the modern history of the Arab world, particularly for his strides towards Arab unity and his anti-imperialist efforts. But his detractors were right to criticise his authoritarianism and his human rights violations.

By the time of these momentous events, Ismail, Youssef and I were no longer in the country. When I finished at Victory College my father sent us all to college in the USA. After three years of being bed-ridden, I had recovered enough to resume a full life, rediscovering the joy of riding my bicycle around the grounds of our home. I had read widely, received a lot of private tuition at home in a range of subjects including English, maths, science, geography and history, and studied hard, passing an external GCE examination at 14. Cambridge, where my father had studied, was not viable as it required students to be at least 18 years old. Whether or not my father foresaw Egypt's dark days or not, he could see that the world was changing rapidly. He instinctively felt that the USA would be a better option for higher education.

• • •

Ismail was 17, Youssef was 16 and I was 14 when we applied to university in the USA. Due to my father's involvement in cotton exporting and textiles, he chose educational institutions within the University of North Carolina system. The then University of North Carolina at Raleigh – renamed North Carolina State

University in 1965 – offered one of the better courses in textile engineering. We received a telegram to confirm that Youssef had been given a place and then everything else followed for the rest of us.

In 1963, Ismail followed Youssef, majoring in business administration at the University of North Carolina at Chapel Hill. I was offered a place at the University of North Carolina at Raleigh to study aeronautical engineering. I wanted to do something different from my brothers and thought I might like to become an aeronautical scientist.

I think I must have been one of the last Egyptian students to whom Nasser granted an exit visa. I was just 15 years old when I arrived in Raleigh. Even without my three years confined to bed at home, I would have been hugely inexperienced. My injury had insulated me even more from any concept of 'real life' and I had little idea of what to expect of a different culture. It was some comfort, of course, that my brothers were there already, but I was still concerned. My father was less worried about grades than about learning more profoundly about life. On the eve of my departure, he told me: 'I expect you to communicate, to inform and to understand other people and cultures and to try to better yourself. Always be tolerant and learn to adapt and understand from your experiences.' Those words are etched in my memory and have guided my life.

The next day, I flew to New York with Charles Hakim, a naturalised American family friend. I stayed with him for about two weeks in Yonkers, New York, and then I travelled on to Raleigh-Durham airport in North Carolina. The flight to New York was only the second time I had been on an aeroplane. (The first time was when I was flown to the UK for leg surgery after my accident.) Back then, Raleigh-Durham airport had a single runway and a small terminal building.

My brothers were supposed to be there waiting for me, but when I got to this tiny airport, they were nowhere to be seen. I remember feeling total trepidation as I checked where Youssef was staying, and I still remember the address. The date stuck too. It was late November 1963, one week after John F. Kennedy was assassinated in Dallas. I had swapped a country in turmoil for one in mourning. The future was uncertain. But it was the era of the American Dream and my life was about to change.

CHAPTER THREE

Adapting to survive

Going to America on my own, aged just 15, was a schoolboy's dream come true. It felt free and wild, with drive-by movies, parties and other social events to go to, and nobody checking what time I arrived home. After a very restricted upbringing in Egypt, I was like a kid in the candy store. But whereas my every need had previously been taken care of by staff and chauffeurs in Egypt, I was suddenly on my own, unmonitored and with no parental oversight. It was, to say the least, liberating. In the 1960s the American Dream was about inspiration and aspiration. It was liberating too, through films, music, books and the alluring American way of life. It was a time of innovation, protest, creativity and rebellion. The Beatles and The Rolling Stones were conquering the USA and I felt I was witnessing and living through a cultural revolution.

When I was still recovering from my accident in Egypt, my father had bought me a red Raleigh bike, which I rode gingerly at first, but gradually gained confidence cycling around our gardens. And now, living in North Carolina, that word, 'Raleigh', again came to represent freedom and adventure.

I quickly settled in the town, joining the FarmHouse fraternity, whose initials referenced 'Faith, Ambition, Reverence, Morality, Honesty, Obedience, Unity, Service and Excellence'. It left out F for 'Fun' and A for 'Anything goes', as I found when I joined this quirky group with its secrets, ceremonies and brotherhood bonding.

Fraternities in American universities date back to 1775 when Phi Beta Kappa was founded at the College of William and Mary in Virginia. It expanded to Harvard and Yale, and it soon spread all over the USA. There are male-only fraternities, female-only sororities, and co-ed groups (also known as 'fraternities') in thousands of colleges where the members make a commitment to each other for life.

For some they are the intersection between dining clubs, literary societies and quaint initiating orders including Masonic lodges. Many have archaic and often absurdly embarrassing initiation rituals. The initiation pledges I had to make every semester were pretty outlandish. Youssef had warned me. One involved being blindfolded and dropped in the middle of nowhere then having to work your way back home on your own. I was sworn to secrecy and it could be a bit scary, but generally the pledges were supposed to be about showing that you had guts. I passed my initiations and was given a fraternity ring.

I loved living in the fraternity's red-brick building on Hillsborough Street, which housed almost thirty of us. We got eggs for breakfast, then maybe chicken for lunch and a burger at dinner, and I became a well-known member of the university's social scene, living a fast-paced life and becoming the fraternity's social committee chairman. My fraternity brothers called me 'Mo', while Ismail was 'Ish' and 'Youssef' was 'Jo'. We were quite popular. I arranged parties and events every weekend with Youssef and my friend James 'Bo' Boedicker; we performed songs at parties as 'Mo, Jo and Bo'. We would belt out Beatles songs, with the so-called 'British invasion' of popular music in full swing. The Beatles played at Raleigh in 1965 and The Rolling Stones supported Patti LaBelle at the Reynolds Coliseum, a sports hall on campus.

This was so different to traditional, conservative Egypt and I loved it. My brothers adapted to the American fraternity way of life in different ways. Youssef fitted in well, but Ismail was homesick, and Yasseen tried to cram a four-year course into two-and-a-half years because he missed the Egyptian way of life. But I felt I had found a people and a place that totally connected with me and made me feel I could prosper. It was brimming with confidence and zest.

I was very happy during those early years. Life was good. I was at least two years younger than most of the other students in my year, relishing the taste of complete liberty for the first time. I had my fraternity brothers and friends and I felt free. I loved basketball and American football; I followed the Washington Redskins and the Baltimore Colts. My favourite player was Johnny Unitas, the Colts' quarterback. Once I got an American driving licence and could drive, I bought a silver 1964 Corvette with Youssef and my cousin Ahmed, who like my brother was also studying chemical engineering at NC State. I felt so at home in the USA. What could possibly go wrong?

I soon found out. My father had been very clear that, beyond a limited stipend, we would all have to earn our own way. He gave us an allowance and I felt no financial worries and always thought that somehow every bill would be paid. My father wrote regularly but his letters were heavily censored and the first we knew of how unstable Egypt had become was when the cotton industry was nationalised and most of our family's wealth confiscated. It was a complete shock and an extraordinarily punitive, even vindictive act that affected all of us. The decree stated that the sequestration applied comprehensively to 'Loutfy Mansour and family'.

Even my father's brother, Mostafa Kamel Mansour, lost his farm. It mattered little to the Egyptian government that he was a famous footballer playing for Cairo-based Al Ahly as well as for the national Egyptian team. He took part in 1934's World Cup in Italy, when Egypt became the first African country to take part (the team did not qualify again for the Finals until 1990). A journalist once quipped that there were 'three miracles in Egypt: the pyramids, the Sphinx and Mostafa Kamel Mansour? Not according to Nasser, who targeted him and us.

It was devastating when the money from my father ceased. In one of the heavily censored letters he wrote to my brothers and me, he told us how his company had been nationalised and his assets seized by the state, which meant no more money could be sent on to us. 'Now you will have to become men,' he wrote, 'because I will no longer be able to support you in college.' He stressed that not even President Nasser, whatever damage he imposed, could take our minds or education from us. We had been receiving $200 a month to pay our rent, food, car payments and clothing bills. But my debt to my fraternity had ratcheted up to $454 – equivalent to about $4,000 today – and even though we traded in the Corvette for a cheap VW Beetle I had no immediate way of paying it back. Later, at our weekly meeting in the frat house I raised my hand and told everyone I was sorry, but I needed to leave the fraternity and would repay every cent I owed. I had tears in my eyes because this was my second family in the USA. My blood-family back in Egypt seemed a long way away. In my culture people would stand with you in difficult times, but this was America and things were different here. I did not know what people would say or do.

Leaving the fraternity lifestyle was a real blow. I think I was the first student ever to resign from the fraternity. More than 50 years later, when I visited the fraternity in Raleigh in 2022, I was amazed to discover that my resignation letter had been kept in a cabinet all those years. It said, simply:

Dear Brothers of FarmHouse,

Due to financial reasons, I find it essential for me to present my resignation as an active brother of FarmHouse. It really was a great benefit for me to be a brother of FarmHouse, and I will always cherish the days I was a member. I hope all of you have the greatest success in life.

Fraternally,

Mo Mansour

Re-reading those words I had written in the 1960s transported me back to what was an intensely sad moment for me. It also called to my mind long-suppressed memories of being deserted by my friends at the age of ten when I had my car accident.

• • •

After leaving the frat house, I found a small and simple home on Chamberlain Street, close to the campus in Raleigh, and Youssef and my cousin Ahmed, as well as former fraternity members Bo, Donald Cline, Clyde Bogle and Ray O'Keeffe, among others, also lived there. My brother Ismail also would visit frequently. This was a small house but we often crammed seven or eight people in there to keep costs down. The rent on my new lodgings was very low at about $20 a month. Donald was a postgraduate student whose father had a chicken farm, so we lived hand to mouth, eating virtually nothing but his family's eggs and unbuttered bread – we couldn't even afford butter – for six months.

I looked for a job, finding minimum wage employment in a small Italian restaurant called Amedeo's, initially as a dishwasher and then as a waiter for $1.25 an hour. I could never have foreseen it but leaving the fraternity and working at Amedeo's turned out to be good for me. The owner was an Italian man called Amedeo Richard DeAngelis, who had previously been an American football player for NC State University, who we nicknamed 'Dick'. He was a big, somewhat intimidating guy who, at first, gave me the toughest, most unappealing jobs. I was always very polite to him, calling him 'Sir', but I have a tough side too and I remember complaining to him once about being treated as a bit of a lackey. 'Son', he said to me, patting me on the back, 'I am teaching you how to work'. Despite Dick's gruff exterior, he liked me and appreciated the hard work that I put in, promoting me to wait on tables and then, later, as head waiter. I think I did well on tips as I always tried to talk nicely with the customers. The average bill was around $3 and tips were usually a quarter. I used to go to the cash register and exchange coins for dollar notes. I scrimped and saved and eventually paid my debts. It made me know the value of money and learn to live within my means. The restaurant, which opened in 1963, still exists on Raleigh's Western Boulevard, though Dick sadly died in 2021. Every time I am in town, I make a pilgrimage there.

Almost thirty years later, when my son Loutfy was at a basketball camp nearby, I took my wife Fafy and my eldest son, Mansour, to Amedeo's where I introduced them to Dick. My old boss had aged since I last saw him but he was exactly the same in spirit. I tipped the waiter $100 and Dick told him: 'See this guy. He is now a wealthy businessman and everything he has learned, he learned from me'. He had a point.

Leaving the fraternity had taught me that money is far from everything in life. It is about character and doing something that is constructive and helps to build something. Working hard so that I could meet my bills and pay off my debts made me take responsibility for my own life and welfare. I would save $3–5 and pay my debts back to the fraternity in small chunks or use it to pay my rent. I saw that nobody was going to make things work out for me except myself. Eventually, I repaid every cent of that $454.

The bigger picture was changing very rapidly too. With America bombing North Vietnam in Operation Flaming Dart in February 1965, the political winds were changing direction in the USA. When the president Lyndon B. Johnson announced a campaign of sustained bombing, my fraternity hollered at the TV that America was going to 'go get them.' Everybody seemed to be so gung-ho at the time. But those feelings did not persist. Over the next three years, a succession of former fraternity brothers changed from clean-cut youths supporting the Vietnam campaign to long-haired and bearded hippies marching for peace. One even went on hunger strike, losing more than 20kg in a bid to avoid being drafted. Others who marched off to war returned as shadows of their former selves. Some did not return at all.

This being the 1960s, drug use around the campus increased. A previously polite and introverted Egyptian kid from a good family whom I knew went completely off the rails. He was thought to have had a bad LSD trip and the university threw him out. A lot of people were using drugs, but I never touched any myself, too afraid to do anything that might take me beyond my control.

Still, it was an era of counterculture, a counter revolution, reacting against the uptight 1950s and I loved it. We watched in awe as humanity made a 'giant leap for mankind' with space travel. *The Flintstones* debuted on TV. The contraceptive pill was commercially produced for the first time. At that time half of America's population was under 18. About 65% of Americans were church-goers. A slice of pizza cost 15 cents. It was only in 1960 that love and rock'n'roll became a way of life. It was a way to cope with the friction the public was feeling towards politicians and the US government. On 28 August 1963, Martin Luther King uttered the words 'I have a dream'. In 1964 Ford Motors' flagship muscle car was launched. Peter Sellers played Dr Strangelove in the 1964 classic of the same name. All this blew the mind of a teenage Muslim boy from the quiet suburbs of Alexandria where the mosque had been part of his routine and the most outré entertainment was soccer or playing on the beach. America was breaking its reins of restraint and youth liberation was in full swing.

There were many temptations and as I partied my grades sank, and in my third year of the engineering course, I almost flunked out. I was either late to class or not attending at all, and my grades were mediocre at best. On one physics course, I was given an F for a grade-point average of only 1.25 when I needed a 2.0. Failing the course meant that I would be kicked out. This was a pivotal moment of my whole time in the USA – and a turning point in my life.

I went to see my physics professor, and pleaded. 'I came here from Egypt, where the government is socialist. If I go back, I have no future. Please give me another chance.' It may have sounded pathetic but somehow struck a chord. I was given a second chance. The professor lectured me on where I was going wrong and what I needed to do to turn things around. He gave me an 'incomplete' mark, essentially offering me more time to finish the course but with strict conditions. I had to attend class at eight o'clock and sit at the front of the lecture hall. If I missed a single lecture, I would receive an F grade. We shook hands on the deal and I felt humbled. I think the professor, whose family came from Poland, knew that if I failed, I would be going back to a country that at that time had its opportunities blighted by politics. He saw that the flame of opportunity would have been snuffed out by my foolishness, laziness and naivety.

I switched my major from aeronautical engineering to textiles. I needed to achieve A and B grades to make up for the damage already done to my grade-point average. It would take a lot of hard work and it was time to man up. I made up those grades and graduated in June 1968. I was only then ready to make great strides in the world having stumbled terribly at the start, physically from my car accident but also while attending my first classes at college. Only through incredibly good fortune was I lucky enough to have been given a second chance.

I returned again to Raleigh in May 2022 to deliver the commencement address at NC State's graduation ceremony and receive an honorary doctorate. Although Dick had passed away by then, the restaurant was still going strong. His daughter, Jill, showed me around the kitchen, and we looked through old photos of her father in his football uniform. How Dick would have loved to have been there to remind me about his own graduate schooling of wiping tables, handing out dishes, taking orders. He would have teased me mercilessly that he was the reason I had become a tycoon with over a hundred restaurants in our group. When I spoke at the commencement address of my amazement that 'Mo the waiter now employs 60,000 people around the world', many in the 20,000-strong crowd stood and applauded. It was a moving moment and I like to think that Dick was looking down on me, with a proud look in his eye. But as to my honorary-doctor status, he would have said being a graduate of Amedeo's was of the same calibre. He always had the last laugh.

As I looked out across the vast arena on that spring day, with my son Loutfy and many of my oldest friends, several of my fraternity brothers, in the audience, I reflected how I had truly struggled as a young man and that second chances from Dick and the professor were my saving grace.

As we drove away from the PNC Arena, I thought to myself how I will always be grateful to the university for the faith it showed in me. I hope the career I went on to have, all the people I have employed, all the people who my foundation have supported, has gone some way to repaying that faith.

ع

CHAPTER FOUR

A fight for life

I so wanted to believe that things could only get better, but I was in for a shock. My graduation year of 1968 became my *annus horribilis*. It was the year when I faced the gravest challenge of my life – one far more severe than being hit by that car at the age of ten or almost flunking out and being sent back to Egypt while studying. Life can turn on a sixpence and my final year at NC State, rather than being an open highway headed to my future, threatened to become more like death row.

By the time I graduated in May 1968, I had already been feeling unwell for a little time. When I spotted traces of blood in my urine, I knew I needed to seek medical advice. My mother was visiting us from Egypt – Youssef and Ahmed were graduating at the same time as me. I found a local doctor through the *Yellow Pages*, and she accompanied me to his clinic. I was shocked by his assessment. Outside his offices, I forgot myself for a moment and exclaimed in front of my mother: 'The f***ing doctor said I have cancer!' My mother, always calm and optimistic by nature, tried her best to reassure me. The doctor was speculating and could not be certain. Yet while I wanted to be positive, I feared the worst. It was the 'Big C', and survival rates at the time were low. I panicked and thought I was going to die. Initially I did nothing. I just waited. And my mother eventually returned to Cairo. I must have thought it would somehow go away.

I certainly tried my best to put it to the back of my mind and focus on the next stage of my academic career. I was due to enrol at the University of North Carolina at Chapel Hill in September for summer classes to help me to prepare for my MBA at Auburn University, Alabama, where I was due to continue my education in 1969. A friend offered to help me move my belongings to a house in Chapel Hill, 30 miles from Raleigh, but as we were carrying my sofa out to a U-Haul truck, I felt a sharp pain in my left side as if I'd been stabbed with a blade. Once again, blood appeared in my urine.

I called the doctor, who ordered me straight to the Rex Hospital in Raleigh. I was admitted and the next day they carried out a non-invasive procedure called a laparoscopy to investigate the cause. The surgeon, Dr John Rhodes Sr, later broke the news I had been dreading, although initially I didn't fully grasp what he was telling me. He said I had a 'malignant tumour', and at first, I naively thought this good news, that it wasn't cancer, just a tumour. But someone soon explained that those things are one and the same.

I could not believe it. I'd nearly lost my leg and been bed-ridden from the age of ten for three years, and now, aged just 20, I had cancer. When I was hit by that car a decade earlier my parents were there to support me during my stay in the hospital and my recovery period at home. This time I was thousands of miles from home. There was no way that Nasser would grant a visa to my father. Indeed, there was little chance that either parent would be able to travel to be with me after my mother had previously been granted an exit visa to watch her children graduate. I felt frightened and alone.

We did our best to keep my parents informed of developments. Reflecting the realities of telecommunications with Egypt at the time, phone calls had to be arranged days, if not weeks, in advance. During one call with my father, panic turned to bitterness. 'Mohamed, you have to trust in God,' he said. But I simply could not believe that I was facing another medical urgency. 'Why me? Why me!?' I kept shouting, and then hung up. Youssef took the telephone from me and tried his best to calm me down.

One of my father's close friends in America, Christine Gallagher, chief of staff to the congressman Harold Cooley, called Dr Rhodes to ask for an update on my condition. Egypt's most senior diplomat in Washington at the time, Dr Ashraf Ghorbal, also phoned the doctor for news, and managed to relay the information back to Egypt.

Dr Rhodes told me he wished to operate in the next few days. My brothers and cousin tried to see as much of me as they could but they were often studying or working elsewhere. Youssef, who had moved to Alabama after graduating from NC State to work for a chemicals company in Opelika, drove back to Raleigh. Ismail travelled to visit from another college in North Carolina. Ahmed, who was studying for his MBA at Columbia University, flew in when he had a spare weekend from New York. But I still felt alone, abandoned even. However, just as I had to be resilient when recovering from the car accident, the experience of facing up to this great challenge built my character.

The surgery involved cutting out my left kidney: while the tumour was malignant, it was the size of a teacup. As draining as the operation was, and with an exhausting recovery period, the good news was that they believed they had cleared my body of any cancer cells.

As I lay recovering in hospital for a week, I feared that I would not be able to continue my studies. After initially sharing my care with a friend of Youssef's, my brothers and Ahmed took turns overseeing my recovery by staying with me. Ismail paused studies for a period to help out too.

After the radiation-therapy course was complete, I needed check-ups every six months. After each all-clear, I felt I had been given a new lease of life. I would then try to put it all to the back of my mind until the next appointment. But every time one was coming up, the fear, anxiety and sleepless nights returned. This continued for five long years as the risk of the cancer returning remained.

The experience changed me. I always pay close attention to what I eat and drink. I feel blessed that I survived the car accident and beat cancer, and have also been able to live such a long and happy life. God had been on my side.

I rarely talk about the cancer, and many of my friends will be learning about it for the first time in these pages. It was very traumatic for me and I will never forget it, but I do try to shut it out. I worry that if I think or talk too much about my illness, that the cancer will come back.

The year of 1968 was one of contrasting omens. While I faced my own destiny, America was facing its own identity challenges with trepidation. At a White House conference on crime, singer and actress Eartha Kitt denounced the Vietnam War to President Johnson.

One image dominated the Vietnam War debate, causing Americans to pause and think, 'What on earth are we doing in that far-off country with so many people dying including thousands of Americans?' A Vietcong officer named Nguyễn Văn Lém was executed by a South Vietnamese police chief. The event made headlines around the world, swaying the American public opinion against the war.

The whole country was jolted when Martin Luther King Jr was shot dead at the Lorraine Motel in Memphis, Tennessee. In response, riots erupted in major American cities, lasting several days. There was dire news as well as optimistic events unfolding across the country, such as when Apollo 6 was launched, the second and last unmanned test flight of the Saturn V launch project. Mass grief covered all of America when JFK's brother, the presidential candidate Robert F. Kennedy, was shot at the

Ambassador Hotel in Los Angeles. Kennedy died from his injuries the next day. It was not an easy political or cultural landscape as I tried to find equilibrium in my own personal life too.

Finally, after almost a year of recuperating in the USA, I did get an opportunity to see my father in Sudan at the very end of the 1960s. I had not seen him since 1964, when he had visited us in Washington, DC, and I had not seen my mother since my diagnosis the previous year.

The meeting was possible because my father had been released from his effective house arrest and allowed to leave Egypt. When Jaafar al-Nimeiry, the president of Sudan, came to Cairo for a meeting of the Arab League in 1969, he asked Nasser to allow my father to travel to Sudan, the large country to the south of Egypt that was once ruled by the British and the Egyptians, in order to begin to reform the country's cotton industry. Nasser disliked my father but reluctantly agreed to let him go.

For a year, my father worked as an adviser to the presidency in Sudan. He was then approached by Sudan's Abu Ella family, Old Victorians who owned the Sudan Cotton Company, a firm that was struggling financially and was ranked the lowest in the country in terms of its cotton exports. They asked my father to run the company and offered him 10% of the equity. Under his control, the company went from being the smallest exporter of cotton to the largest as measured by cotton bale exports.

Seeing my father in Sudan was the best possible tonic for me after all my health problems. He sent me a cheap airline ticket – so inexpensive that I would have to take a circuitous route from

Raleigh-Durham to the Sudanese capital of Khartoum via New York, London and Beirut. But while at London Heathrow waiting for my flight to Beirut, I spotted an Egyptair counter and felt such a pang of homesickness that I spontaneously decided to see if I could change my ticket and fly to Sudan via Cairo.

I transferred my luggage, got on the plane without even thinking and landed back on home soil that evening. My onward flight to Khartoum was not until early the following morning so I went to the transit area. It was late by the time I arrived, and I was greeted by an eerie scene. All the windows were blacked out because of the ongoing War of Attrition between Israel, Egypt, Jordan and Syria. It was late and, being the only passenger waiting there, I was approached by a cleaner who asked for a cigarette. I had bought my father a case of Camels but gave the cleaner a packet. In return, I asked him to call my aunt Dawlat Maghraby, my mother's sister, to tell her of my whereabouts. A few minutes later, I was approached by a soldier who asked if I was Egyptian. I was nervous as my family was blacklisted by Nasser at this time. He said an immigration officer wanted to see me. 'Mansour,' he said, looking at my passport. 'Are you related to Khaled Mansour?' 'He's my cousin,' I replied. He asked me to describe Khaled Mansour's appearance. Not seeming to trust my description of my own cousin, the soldier started barking at me about military service and that I would have to go to an army compound.

I was terrified as I didn't know what would happen to me. Some of my friends who had been drafted had not been allowed to leave Egypt for eight years. The officer first took me into a long tunnel underneath that was lit by a single light bulb, then into an office where a general was sitting in full uniform. He asked if I knew Dr Amin El Maghraby and I said he was married to my mother's sister. 'I am married to his sister,' he replied. He told me to call my aunt Dawlat and get her to collect me because I wasn't allowed to travel to Sudan or to go back to America. I told him that I was exempt from national service due to my leg injury and that I had to go back to university for my MBA. He called my aunt, who took me to her house in Cairo. Although the general had prevented me being taken by the military, I was now stuck in Egypt.

I remained in the country for five months as I awaited the results of a medical exam to confirm how I was unfit to serve in the military and, as I sought to gain an exit visa to return to America, my uncle Mostafa worked tirelessly on my behalf. Exploiting his fame as a former footballer and coach, he had access to senior officials in the government. But as impressed as they were to meet him, they always refused to grant me an exit visa.

Although I ended up being stranded in Egypt and missed the chance to see my father in Sudan, I was surrounded by my mother, cousins, aunts and uncles. It was the best possible therapy. The doctors in America were very professional but had always been so blunt, never wanting to sugar-coat bad news. Now I was surrounded by people who loved me and assured me that everything would be fine.

Finally, in the summer of 1970, the last months of Nasser's life, I was granted a visa and flew back to the USA. Soon after Nasser, who by this time was also Egypt's prime minister, suffered a heart attack at the end of an Arab League Summit, and died at the age of 52. He had been in power for 14 years as Egypt's second president, following the revolution of 1952, and his death marked the end of an era. I heard the news after giving a speech at a Chamber of Commerce event in Alabama, and I can truly say that my overriding emotion was one of tremendous relief. I hoped that things would change for the better in Egypt.

Five million people took to the streets of Egypt for Nasser's funeral procession. While Nasser was glorified for his populist achievements, his successor Anwar Sadat, who had been at Nasser's bedside when he died, proved a much more balanced leader who never got the credit he deserved for moving Egypt out of its socialist era, ushering in a more capitalist system that attracted foreign investment. He showed great courage by signing a peace deal with the Israeli prime minister, Menachem Begin, in 1978 when most other Arab countries would not countenance it. He was awarded the Nobel Peace Prize but was assassinated in 1981, and did not receive the same rapturous acclaim that had been given to Nasser at his funeral.

• • •

Studying for my MBA changed everything for me because business turned out to be what I liked and a very natural thing for me. I had spent years watching my father make decisions, which meant I often knew exactly what my MBA professor was going to say before he opened his mouth. I came from a business family and a commercial background, and in contrast to the struggles I had initially experienced at NC State, my grade-point average at

Auburn was now more or less straight A's. I did so well here that following my graduation, I was offered a role in the faculty as an instructor.

In 1971, my yo-yo life between East and West, particularly America and Egypt, brought me another opportunity to see my father, who I had now not seen for so long. We were to meet in London with Rawya and Yasseen.

During our time in the UK, my father took us all by train for a day trip to Cambridge, where he had been an undergraduate. We visited his dorm, met his old tutor and reminisced about his days rowing on the Cam. He loved the architecture and history of St John's College, which was founded in 1511 and boasts among its alumni no fewer than 12 Nobel Prize recipients, seven British prime ministers and 12 archbishops of different countries. He was in his element there, taking us through its distinctive Great Gate adorned with the arms of its founder, Lady Margaret Beaufort. It was wonderful after so many traumatic experiences to be reunited with my father again. I returned to Auburn completely revived.

I linked academic pursuits with business when I joined up with one of my professors, Harold Pickle, to work for a firm he formed called ABC Consulting. We provided advice to small businesses in Alabama with financial problems. We received a grant from the federal government and my natural forte for marketing and finance advice was unearthed. I developed a questionnaire to help businesses ranging from mom-and-pop shops to big factories to identify their problems.

For two years, I criss-crossed Alabama helping about seventy businesses. We suggested solutions, and while some firms simply blamed banks for not giving them enough money, usually some kind of mismanagement needed tackling or a good marketing plan and/or restructuring was needed. The funniest issue I encountered was a funeral home that complained that business was declining because people were no longer dying at the same rate. We all laughed at that one but did not take it seriously as a cause of the firm's decline.

After so many struggles in Raleigh, I lived well and happily in Alabama. I acquired a Dobermann pinscher called Fahd – Egyptian for 'leopard', because it was dark and sleek. I rode my bicycle everywhere with Fahd trotting alongside. American students called him 'Faddy' because they could not pronounce his name. Sadly, when I left America in 1973, I had to leave Fahd behind, gifting him to my neighbours. He was so loyal to me that he refused to eat and died soon after I had departed. I have never had a pet since.

Some 25 years later in 1997, one of the students I taught became head of a big Alabama bank. He saw my name in *Forbes* magazine and told the dean of the business school at Auburn who asked me to visit the university. I came from Cairo and retraced my steps to the two-bedroom, 50sq.m apartment at 7 East Drake Avenue, which I shared with Youssef and my cousin Sherif. It looked smaller than I remembered. They asked me to teach the same class as I had done, and their university magazine published a piece about it accompanied by some photos of me, including one that was taken with the president George H.W. Bush during a visit to Egypt. The dean and president of the university invited me for a dinner in my honour at their home. It was very touching and brought back some great memories.

America stamped its mark on the Mansour family. Youssef stayed in America for 12 years, falling in love with Mary Mosely, from Montgomery, Alabama, who had worked as my secretary at ABC Consulting. They married and had a daughter, Amina, before moving back to Egypt in 1976, separating years later. Ismail stayed until 1969, while I was there for a decade.

In 1972, my father wanted Youssef and me to come to London. We had a joyous dinner together in Mayfair but the next morning he was shocked to learn from the Sudanese ambassador that the cotton industry in Sudan had been nationalised. President al-Nimeiry, who had invited my father to reform his country's cotton industry, had joined another wave of socialism sweeping over the Middle East, facilitating the rise of Colonel Gaddafi in Libya and Hafez al-Assad in Syria. Like Nasser before them, their regimes were all strongly supported by the Soviet Union.

The Sudanese leader was a military officer who came to power after a military coup in 1969. He established a one-party state, with his Sudanese Socialist Union as the sole legal political entity, and began to follow Nasser's example by nationalising most of the private sector. It was just our luck that all our financial future at that time turned out to be in his hands.

It seemed impossible that lightning could strike us twice. We found my father completely devastated, almost in tears. 'What do

I do now?' he asked us. 'My business was taken from me in Egypt and now exactly the same thing has happened in Sudan.' In Egypt, he had been number one and in Sudan, he had successfully taken the cotton business from 40th to that same top position in just a year. Spinning mills and factories across the world respected his name, knowing that he was a man of his word. I said: 'Dad, why are you working in this part of the world? Why not work out of Europe?' He flew to Switzerland the next day to explore the feasibility of yet another move.

Everything of my family's assets had been confiscated. My father still had some money in Egypt but no hard currency in foreign exchange. He met with some old friends in Geneva, including an Egyptian called Clement Cohen, who had created a cotton brokerage called Cottonuvers, and he gifted my father a rent-free office. Instead of selling Sudanese cotton, he started to broker it, acting as a middleman between state-owned cotton farms and spinning mills across the globe. Within two years, he became the world's largest buyer of Sudanese cotton.

Meanwhile, as President Sadat attempted to open up Egypt, he allowed my father to return home to work. This led to my father asking me to return to Egypt to work with him and Ismail in exporting Sudanese cotton in 1973. I would probably have liked another year at Auburn, but I could not say no to my father.

I joined the company of Loutfy Mansour and Sons, alongside my father, Ismail and an accountant. After a decade apart, it was touching to be with him again. I loved working with my father in the daytime, and then in the evenings, Ismail and I would head into central Alexandria for the best food in town at fashion-able spots like the Italian restaurant Santa Lucia, the Pam-Pam nightclub and the Windsor Palace hotel.

There were only four of us working at the cotton brokerage. My father ran the company, a bookkeeper did the accounts and Ismail and I did everything else. But it was not all plain sailing and sometimes I felt he did not give me enough responsibility or respect. I was my father's driver and tea man. I had left Egypt at 15 having completed my education, created my own company, flour-ished at business school and worked as a teacher. My father had not seen that, and at times treated me as if I were a child.

This was a volatile period to be at home, especially with Egypt, Jordan and Syria fighting Israel in the Yom Kippur War of 1973. When members of OPEC proclaimed an oil embargo to hurt nations perceived as supporting Israel, oil prices surged, which had a knock-on effect of increasing the cost of synthetic fibres like nylon and polyester. Cotton prices rocketed. We had committed to buy cotton at 32 cents per ounce and the sale price quickly rose to over 100 cents. We made millions of dollars in a very short time span. 'I have spent my entire life in the cotton industry, and I have never known anything like this,' my father told me. 'Mohamed, you are good luck, you know. You have only just joined the business and look at what is happening.'

The price of cotton peaked at 132 cents. I thought the pros-pects for the business must be fantastic, but my father did not believe that the high levels were sustainable. By March 1974, the price of oil was up from $3 to nearly $12 a barrel, but it was clear that the West would not allow the price to keep rising indefinitely. I wanted to carry on, but my father said we should sell all our holdings over the next year. He refused to buy cotton for future seasons, taking only a very small quota, and his caution proved absolutely correct as the cotton price plummeted to 50 cents. My father had anticipated the rise-and-fall market correctly, while others were burned.

The experience convinced my father, then aged 65, that his sons should get into a different sector. 'You need something more long term,' he told us. With oil even more volatile than cotton, it seemed odd that the sector he chose for us was the automotive industry. But that was to take my brothers and me on a fast and exciting road.

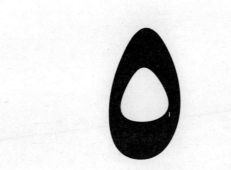

CHAPTER FIVE

'Mr Mansour Chevrolet'

In July 1976, my world fell apart. My father had just returned from a trip to the USA when he received the awful news that my sister's father-in-law, who was a dear friend to my father, had been in a serious car accident. His wife was staying in our house when my father woke me up to ask me to take her and her son to see his friend in the hospital. By the time we reached the hospital, his friend had died. We drove with his wife alongside the hearse back to Alexandria, where he was laid to rest.

When we returned home, my father was waiting for us on the grand staircase at the front of the building and hugged us. He was shaken and grief-stricken. We had dinner and then he went to his favourite place on the second-floor balcony, where he liked to sit and talk politics with his friends. I asked if he needed anything, kissed his hand and retired to my quarters on the third floor. From my bedroom window I looked out and thought I caught sight of him in the garden, sitting at a table. I often think back to that apparent sighting of him outside, and what it meant. Maybe it was an illusion, or maybe I imagined it, because I'd just left him on his bedroom balcony on the opposite side of the house.

Moments later there was a knock at my door and Zakiya, Ismail's wife, was standing there. 'Mohamed. Please come down, your father is not well,' she said. We rushed to the balcony where we found my father in his chair. He was taken to hospital and placed in intensive care.

He was in a coma for two weeks. He briefly revived and I got a call and rushed to his hospital bedside. When I arrived, I was so happy when I saw him awake and kissed his hand. He asked how I was, enquired after a business deal that we had been working on and told me he was going to sleep. It was the last thing he ever said to me. Very peacefully he breathed his last.

The doctors concluded that my father had died of a brain haemorrhage, possibly brought on by high blood pressure caused by stress. His funeral in Alexandria was attended by thousands of people, ranging from Egyptian dignitaries and farmers, to drivers and distributors, who travelled from the towns and villages of rural Egypt to pay their respects in a huge marquee beside our house. These were the people he loved. Every Friday, he would go to the mosque and give some money to them. Even after losing all his assets under Nasser's rule, he continued doing it, even when my mother told him that she didn't know how they were going to eat the next day. 'You give to the poor, you get it back,' he would tell us. 'You do good in life, you get good back.'

There is not a day that goes by when I do not think about him or my mother. I was determined to repay my father's personal faith in me, which is something that still drives my passion for growth in my personal and business life today. He had singled me out about a year before his death, giving me power of attorney over the family's financial affairs and to sign deals on his behalf. The wealth he had made was entrusted to me to administer on behalf of the family.

The next stage in my life was a ride dominated and defined by cars. It was not exactly 0–60mph in ten seconds but it was our family's economic highway for success, which has continued for more than half my lifetime. We went from not knowing exactly what we were doing – making costly errors that ranged from ordering a shipment of people-carriers without any seats to naivety in managing foreign currency risks – to being twenty-first-century pioneers for electric cars in Africa and hopefully beyond.

The auto industry in Egypt had been nationalised following the revolution of 1952. After some initial setbacks for state-produced vehicles including the ill-fated Ramses automobile, which was affected by poor design and performance, in 1960 the government established the Nasr car company, which manufactured Fiat vehicles and had a monopoly over the automotive market until President Sadat's reforms in the early to mid-1970s.

America's biggest car manufacturers, General Motors (GM) and Ford, had operated in Egypt prior to 1952. GM had a network of dealers across the country including dealerships in Cairo and

Alexandria operated by Egypt's Magar brothers. All those businesses were nationalised under the Nasser administration. But by 1975, Sadat was ready for car imports from the private sector to restart. The market was small, but there would still be huge interest in the new franchises for the large USA and European manufacturers.

My father was keen to diversify his business and sensed an opportunity in the automotive industry. He had always loved cars. Throughout my childhood, he owned a Pontiac and several Chevrolets. Once he bought a Mercedes in Geneva and we took a road trip in it from Switzerland to Trieste, Italy, where it was shipped to Egypt. My father had heard that GM wanted to shake things up and were looking for new distributors to Egypt. He sat down with GM executive Jack Lawrence in 1975, and the meeting changed everything. The cotton traders were going into the car business. Jack, a highly respected executive within GM, oversaw our region. He knew next to nothing of my father but quickly discovered his reputation as a man to trust. He liked my father for three other reasons: his companies possessed financial strength, he had three USA-educated sons and, with my father aged 65, succession seemed secure. Under Sadat, Egypt, previously allied to the Soviet Union, had opened its doors to American trade. We were lucky to be in the right place at the right time.

In December 1975, my father reached an agreement with GM, a deal that has proved momentous for our family. My father, siblings and I set up the business with a modest amount of capital. The big USA banks like Citibank and Chase Manhattan were moving back into the country but were cautious about lending to support import businesses. Our properties and other personal assets were put up as collateral to secure the necessary letters of credit.

GM operated several brands at the time – Chevrolet, Bedford, Isuzu, Buick, Oldsmobile, Pontiac and Cadillac among them. My father was given the Chevrolet brand, while the Magar brothers were able to re-enter the market after being given the rights to Pontiac and Buick. But there was a catch. Back in America, it was customary for authorised GM dealers to compete rather than collaborate, and GM wanted this model for Egypt. This meant we would be competing with other GM dealers, as well as dealers of other manufacturers. GM also wanted us to set up different branches of our own business and suggested we name them after my father, my siblings and me. It was a structure that would cause problems for us further down the road.

As my father lived and worked in Alexandria, our solution was to create a holding company, located in the city's tax-efficient 'free zone', called Loutfy Mansour Automobile Trading Company (LMATC). LMATC in effect would hold the power, as it would arrange the trade financing with the banks, purchase the vehicles from GM, import them into Egypt on a duty-free basis, and then sell them on to the three local companies, which would pay taxes on the vehicles they sold. Loutfy Mansour Trading, operated by my father, was set up in the LMATC office in Alexandria; Mohamed Motors, which I took charge of, covered Cairo; and Ismail Engineering, which my older brother Ismail managed, covered Upper Egypt. (Youssef had taken a job in Saudi Arabia with an investment company owned by our cousin, Ahmed.) In the 1980s Yasseen joined the automotive business, helping me to run the company until he left to set up our McDonald's business in the 1990s.

There was understandable caution and a lack of risk-taking within the nascent private sector in Egypt in the 1970s. Many founders and entrepreneurs, worried that what had happened under Nasser could happen again, lacked the confidence to invest, and the economy was slow to expand. The country's financial system and infrastructure were under-developed. Importers had to buy dollars and other foreign currencies from unregulated trading firms, which caused the Egyptian pound to lose value as demand for dollars grew. The conditions could hardly be judged to be ripe for a new imports-based business venture that would be buying from a manufacturer in US dollars and selling them to consumers in Egyptian pounds.

However, despite losing two of his businesses to governments, my father knew that the political tide had turned and was fully committed to the new venture. One of his most visionary moves was to lease a Ford facility in Alexandria, converting it into a GM showroom, service station and parts outlet. That decision enabled us to enter the market more rapidly. We later bought the former Ford facility outright. My father then completed our very first order – for 20 pick-up trucks from GM in the USA.

The agreement with GM showed huge foresight on my father's part, but none of us appreciated how dominant the motor car was going to become in Egypt or just what an amazing opportunity we had been given. My father thought if things went well, we could net maybe E£50,000 a year in profits. We did not foresee the effects of mass industrialisation on Egypt, followed then by globalisation. This would turn into the proverbial yellow brick road for us.

But when my father passed away in July 1976, the business was less than a year old and we were still just getting started. Sales were small – and GM was worried about the future of the company under new management. We had learned from the best, but my brothers and I were different to my father as businesspeople. Years of battling to build and rebuild his cotton empire had taught my father the soft skills of how to make friends and build long-lasting business relations. He was a consummate salesman.

One of the last deals that he worked on played very much to his strengths, rather than ours. Following Sadat's reforms, Washington pledged aid to Egypt through the United States Agency for International Development (USAID). Under the programme, USAID agreed to fund infrastructure investment on the basis that USA exporters (like GM) would benefit. The Egyptian government wanted to upgrade the public transportation network in Cairo, and issued two tenders, one to supply buses to the city, the other to supply trucks to carry wheat, grain and other commodities for the Ministry of Supply, the department responsible for food security. The combined value of the contracts was an estimated $70 million (around $350 million in today's money). The supplier of the vehicles would benefit the most, but my father's company, acting as an agent, would take 1%. Thanks to our relationship with GM, my father thought we had a good chance of success. He travelled constantly to GM's headquarters in Detroit. But when he passed away, the government awarded the contracts to other bidders. My brothers and I did not have the knowledge or experience to act as intermediaries, and the government probably knew it. From that day on, we focused solely on being dealers, rather than agents.

GM knew our father, but for the company, the sons were untested. It was a difficult moment for the new business relationship. GM sent a team of executives to attend the funeral: officially, as a mark of respect to my father; unofficially, to test our mettle. In our culture, it is customary to leave people alone during the mourning period, but they pointedly asked me a lot of questions about the plans for the business.

The future of the new business was uncertain. Youssef agreed to return to Egypt and took over the Chevrolet dealership in Alexandria that my father had set up. I continued to manage Cairo and Ismail remained in charge of the south.

I had a new plan. It was a simple step-by-step initiative: keep the money inside the company. 'Listen,' I told my brothers, 'we are going to import two cars and sell them. Then, we will import four and sell them. After that, eight. Every time, we will keep the money in the business.' We focused on Alexandria – Cairo could wait. This was a turning point until we were on an even keel. I knew that we could make a success of the enterprise this way. Gradually, we learned about our home market and its growing demand for motor vehicles; which models could be successful and how to market them to our nation's upwardly-mobile population.

The questions from GM kept coming. They were becoming impatient and wanted to know when Mohamed Motors was going to launch. I was living in Alexandria at the time and began to commute to Cairo. Joining me on those long journeys to and from Alexandria was my dear friend Adel Khadr, who was one of the first five employees at Mohamed Motors. I initially met him through his brother, an old friend at Victoria College called Abdel Aziz Khadr, the school's head boy who graduated top of his class and later went on to study engineering at the University of Alexandria. Adel worked his way up through the business and was made CEO in 1994, a position he held until his retirement in 2021. We worked closely together – even though I was running Mantrac, our Caterpillar dealership, by that time, he and I would speak as I was driven to the Mantrac office in the morning and at the end of the day, and we would meet often during the day in my office. I trusted him with the day-to-day operations of the company while I set the strategic direction of the business. That model still works well with his successor Ankush Arora, who joined us in 2014 and took over as CEO in summer 2021. Ankush, who is bright and energetic, is taking the company forward.

Those days of commuting from Alexandria to Cairo were long and tiring, with at least six hours spent travelling between the two cities. After about six months of commuting, I decided to move to Cairo permanently. I said goodbye to my mother, drove to the capital and rented an apartment in a building where Rawya lived. I developed friendships in the city and began to enjoy life there. I was a bachelor, and I enjoyed it. I'd work from ten o'clock in the morning to one o'clock in the afternoon, break for a siesta, and then work another shift from about four o'clock until nine o'clock in the evening, and then go and meet friends for dinner and dancing in downtown Cairo.

The lines between my work–life balance blurred. I had chosen to employ people I either knew personally or who came from families that I knew and respected. These recruits were roughly the same as me – similar in age, educated, Egyptian – and would go on to become my friends. It was a good decision to hire them. At the time, most people in the country who had experience of working in the auto industry had been civil servants, as the industry had been nationalised under Nasser. I wanted people who were smart, ambitious and driven. It did not matter if they had little to no experience of the auto. Those people who we hired would grow with us and go on to be the core team of Mansour Chevrolet. Initially, though, the dynamic was wrong. I had an open-door policy, and the atmosphere was collegiate but a tipping point came when I found my colleagues playing football in the yard rather than doing their jobs. I had to draw the line. I told them this was no way to do business and I closed the door to my office, to create some distance. We would still go out together in the evenings, but work was work and play was play.

I learned from my father that word of mouth alongside our promise and reputation are the most important qualities. If you commit to something, you have to deliver it – and do it better than any of your competitors. We started with 20–30 cars to sell each year and even though I agreed to GM giving us an annual target of 50, I felt we could achieve 100. I preferred to under-promise and over-deliver. In Egypt, it is common to claim that you can sell 500 but end up only achieving 100. People regularly overshoot and under-deliver in Egypt. There's a saying in Egypt that effectively means if something can be done tomorrow, all is well, but if it can't be, never mind.

More than forty years later, I keep to the mantra of 'under-promise and over-deliver' whenever I am asked how many units of something I am planning to sell. If I have 100 in mind, I will say I can sell 50 or 70. And in the year after that, I will be planning to sell 300 or 400. This is how we started, and it is how we continue to grow the business today. (By 2021 our sales were around 100,000.)

We learned as we went. We didn't realise that if we wanted to sell minivans for passenger use, we would have to order the pas-senger seats as extras. Our sales manager found this out the hard way when we arranged financing for what turned out to be, essen-tially, 36 empty vans. To make them viable products and thus, crucially, be able to repay the loans, we had to find a welder, give him a design and get the seats made locally. We pulled it off but it was a worrying moment for our young business. On another occa-sion, we ordered some trucks that were too big for Egypt's narrow roads. They didn't sell and we had to bring in smaller pick-up trucks. Our mistakes were due to inexperience but were costly in terms of our time and money.

We faced stiff competition despite being the country's only authorised dealer. We discovered 17 other companies around the country that claimed to be authorised dealers for Chevrolet, selling cars they had imported from Saudi Arabia. It was like the Wild West. To combat such operators, we needed to do more to position ourselves with the public as the number one Chevrolet dealer. I wanted us to be as synonymous with GM cars as McDonald's is with hamburgers.

We alighted on a sales promotion that helped us grow significantly – and even led us to change our name. Football was the key. In the 1970s, European football teams began emblazoning logos on their shirts, so I proposed getting the Mohamed Motors marque printed on the jerseys of Al Ahly, Egypt's best-supported football club. It was a perfect fit. Probably 70% of Egyptian football fans supported this team, and the players wear red, like Manchester United. This was likely the first deal of its kind ever struck in Egypt. I agreed to pay around $22,000 for the rights. It was a brilliant deal for our brand's recognition. To get the logo on the shirts was not as simple as you might think, and we had to outsource the printing to a company in Brazil that could do it, which meant flying someone out to South America and back to get the shirts stamped with our logo.

But what if Al Ahly lost their first match with the Mohamed Motors name on their shirts? I thought to myself. Egyptians are very superstitious, and I knew that a defeat would upset the fans, our prospective customers, and may harm the brand. There was already a backlash in some newspapers to the very idea of sponsor logos on football jerseys, so we were taking a calculated risk with the campaign. As an incentive to the team, we offered performance-related bonuses to the players including E£500 per player if the team won the first crucial match with our logo. We need not worry – this was an excellent Al Ahly team line-up, they won 3-0 on the day and went on to win the league and cup.

Fans of the club began asking themselves who Mohamed Motors were. Once it became clear that the 'Mohamed' in the name referred to me, the fans started to call us 'Mansour Chevrolet', while I became known as 'Mr Mansour Chevrolet'. The club won the league again the following year. By the end of the 1970s GM had authorised a change in the name of the company from Mohamed Motors to Mansour Chevrolet Company.

The marketing boost was enormously beneficial. Nowadays, of course, the figures involved in such deals are far higher – in 2012, for example, Chevrolet itself signed a $559 million seven-year sponsorship deal with Manchester United in the English Premier League. Mansour Chevrolet became a household name and from then onwards we were known across Egypt as the only authorised GM dealers selling the Chevrolet brand. The game of soccer was the catalyst and the sponsorship of Al Ahly was a game changer. It would not be the last time that football would feature in the success of our business.

We wanted to diversify, and the kernel of an idea began to form when I attended a GM conference in Greece in the late 1970s. Someone was selling a smaller and cheaper pick-up made in Japan that sported a Chevrolet logo. I had to look twice. The vehicle was made by Isuzu, a Japanese company in which General Motors had a 38% stake, but it was branded with the Chevrolet badge. This was exactly what Egypt needed; an economical pick-up to compete with the Toyota and Nissan vehicles that were dominant in Egypt at the time. We found that 93 of these vehicles were classed as 'ex-factory', shipped elsewhere but not sold. We ordered them directly from Isuzu in Japan, complete with the Chevrolet badge. The 93 vehicles we imported in this way were snapped up almost immediately and that took our automotive journey in a brand-new direction.

This model allowed us to take advantage of the boom in Japanese vehicles prevalent during the 1980s. Nissan, Toyota and Mazda were seeing their UK and continental European sales take off. This was a new phenomenon. Britain had its Bedford vans and trucks, while America had Buick and Cadillac. These were the vehicles that everybody strived to drive. But Japanese motor manufacturers had been making inroads into these markets in the 1960s and 1970s. They were generally less expensive than their European and American counterparts and the quality was improving. This was a trend we could follow and eventually lead. We started to order increasing numbers of Chevrolet-branded vehicles from Isuzu and by 1984, we had become the largest Isuzu dealer in the world, having ordered and sold more than 14,000 vehicles.

There were times when my values came under pressure, and I had to be careful in ensuring that I was taking the right path. One of the hardest decisions I ever had to make was to lay off hundreds of people in the 1980s when our business was facing bankruptcy.

There was a number of contributing factors. Firstly, we were inexperienced in how to structure and manage debt. When we financed the imports from Detroit, we generally borrowed in US dollars. Our cars were then sold to our corporate and individual customers in Egyptian pounds. This approach worked well while the Egyptian pound remained strong compared to the dollar. But we failed to recognise the degree to which we were exposed to substantial risk in the event that the Central Bank of Egypt was instructed to intervene and devalue the currency to boost exports and protect domestic producers against foreign competitors. We were reliant on importing products from overseas. Our business had an Achilles heel.

We had grown up accustomed to the strength of the Egyptian currency. In 1960 it was one of the strongest currencies in the world, worth more than the US dollar and the British pound, and other associated currencies such as the Kuwaiti dinar. Some air was taken out of the currency's ballooning strength in a devaluation in 1963, which reduced its value so that one dollar was the equivalent of about E£0.4. But from the late 1970s, the story has been one of steady decline, periods of relative stability punctuated by declines in the value of the Egyptian currency. During the 1980s and 1990s, the value declined to about E£3 to every dollar, and there were further falls in the early 2000s, eventually steadying at about E£6 to the dollar. Every time the Egyptian pound weakened against the dollar, we paid the price. The cost of servicing our debt and purchasing vehicles became more expensive.

Globalisation and mass industrialisation were on the horizon, and I felt that we could make a seismic difference if we could operate our own factory making Chevrolet-branded vehicles in Egypt. We had been talking to GM and the GM-backed Isuzu about building a factory from the late 1970s, but large corporations can be very slow moving, and it was not until 1983 that we broke ground on the facility. We believe the GM Egypt factory was the first to be established in Egypt for a multinational company. It was set up as a joint venture with our company, GM, Isuzu and a number of minority shareholders, with the GM/Isuzu block holding 51% control. We invested heavily in the new venture at a time in the early 1980s when nobody wanted to invest in Egypt. It was not a business-friendly nation; there was a lot of red tape, which made it difficult to get things done.

By the time the factory was built, Egypt was in the midst of another economic crisis that saw the Egyptian pound fall greatly in value once again. The government moved swiftly in issuing a decree stopping all imports to protect the currency. All imports in transit were stopped at the border. We had between 3,000 and 4,000 vehicles in a 'free zone' just outside Alexandria. The cars were essentially in a segregated zone that was not considered to be a part of Egypt for tax purposes. They had made it into the zone without paying duty but were not allowed to leave the country. So, from 1985, for three years these vehicles were stuck in no-man's land. We could not move them nor sell them anywhere but we still had to pay Isuzu for them.

The government's policy meant that only new cars that had been made locally could be sold in the country, and our factory's production line would not be operating until 1988. We had paid for those cars, paid the interest on their purchase to our banks but we could not bring them to our dealerships to sell as we could not import from the free zone. After we finally obtained a permit to bring them in, we had to sell them at discounts of between 40 and 60% as they had aged. For three years, our revenue plummeted as if diving from a cliff. We were the only GM parts business in the country but allowing for sales from that unit, our revenues collapsed by about 90%.

We came under huge pressure from our banks. My father used to say that banks give you an umbrella when the sun is shining and take it back when the rain comes down. The tone of our conversations went from warm and jovial to: 'Mr Mansour, when are you going to pay?' Irrespective of what returns the company could generate, we were forced to reschedule our commitments with banks, cover foreign exchange losses and give assets as guarantees. We had approximately 1,200 employees, but we had no alternative but to sell assets and make redundancies. About a third of our people had to be let go. There were days when I would leave the office and not know what tomorrow would bring because the outlook was so grim.

We stuck it out, using every cent we had made in the 1970s from the cotton or automotive businesses to repay our loans. We spent all the money my father had left to my mother and plunged every cent we could afford into the business. We still fell some way short of covering all our debts, but the banks could see that we were doing all that we could.

Our Alexandria base became the amalgamated company headquarters, and my family and I moved out of our rental home in Cairo to my mother's house in Alexandria. Doing so not only enabled me to work out of the new headquarters but it also helped to reduce expenses and demonstrate to staff that we were all in this together. My brothers and I agreed to waive all dividends while the crisis was ongoing; indeed we did not restart distributing profits to the shareholders – who were my brothers, my sister and me – until the mid-1990s, by which time we had cleared our losses and built a capital buffer.

Being back in Alexandria allowed me to look more closely at the financial records for the different companies. It was a very complex picture as I had to look through four financial statements, records systems and governance structures. One company was down, another was up, it was very confusing. Most of the records were on paper – it was the 1980s and we had yet to become fully computerised. I regularly worked late into the evening trying to understand the current picture and consider the best approach for the future.

We were offered deals to financially engineer ourselves out of the crisis, borrowing more or bringing in private equity partners, but I felt that we were not in that kind of business. It was not until 1996 that we started lowering our debt ratio. We hung in there, reducing our costs, negotiating with our banks for extended repayment periods, selling assets and using our private wealth to pay off the debts.

However desperate things became, we were able to draw some confidence from the recognition that we had completed the restructuring and our factory would eventually be finished. We just had to get through the next year or two and then we would be on stronger ground. We could see the light at the end of the tunnel. But, as a result of the pressure, I endured many sleepless nights.

On days when the weight of all this was dragging me down, I would drive to Alexandria to visit my mother. I would visit her, feeling very low, saying that I did not think there was any way that we could continue. But she would tell me how she and my father trusted me and knew that I could turn it around. After talking to her, I always left feeling like a lion, ready to take on the world again.

Our financial troubles coincided with a terrible family crisis in 1990. My dear brother, Ismail, suffered a devastating brain haemorrhage and fell into a coma. We wanted to do everything we could for him and considered whether it would be feasible to fly him from Cairo to the world-leading Johns Hopkins Hospital in Baltimore in the USA. I didn't think we had the money, but Youssef said that we could just about find the necessary amount to cover the costs.

My brothers and I remained at Ismail's bedside for many months. Ismail, who was married with three children, remained unwell for seven years. He passed away at the age of 53 in Cairo in 1997. His two sons are now involved in the family business, carrying on his legacy. It is more than 25 years since his passing, and I still miss him terribly.

Our auto business still had many issues to deal with. After our factory started production, dealers that were used to importing started receiving its products from GM and used these to compete directly with us. We built service stations, invested in facilities, imported parts and did everything we could to give after-sales service, but we did not have any passenger cars and were at a natural disadvantage to the other dealerships that did.

Whatever the factory produced for Chevrolet, we would try to sell, but other vehicles came out with Bedford and Isuzu logos, for example, and were supplied to other dealers who tried to undercut us.

It was clear to us that the multi-dealer model was broken. Mom-and-pop outlets were caught in a vicious cycle as prices became depressed and they were not able to earn enough to restock their inventory. We wanted to compete with the dealers of other manufacturers, not other GM dealers. A turning point came in January 1998, when we were able to secure an exclusive agreement with Opel, the then GM-owned German car manufacturer. The success we made of the Opel business demonstrated what was possible once we were free of the shackles of the multi-dealer system.

In 1999, the whole economy went into recession, as a real-estate bubble burst. Other dealers started to falter, going bankrupt while also owing GM significant sums. Production at GM Egypt was severely impacted by the declining market, and as shifts were reduced, workers went on strike. We stepped in, taking a financial hit, and guaranteed that production at the factory for the next three months would continue, in effect bailing out GM Egypt. GM was so impressed that it dispatched a team to Egypt to investigate the feasibility of giving us sole exclusivity over the Egyptian market. They became increasingly receptive to our proposal and finally agreed that going forward we would be the only GM dealership, using the Opel agreement as a measure of our successes in this area.

It is hard to understate how significant this deal was for us, and indeed for GM, which had set a precedent and torn up a decades-long policy. By 2006 we were the largest GM dealer in the world, excluding China, and even today we remain one of the largest globally. Roughly one in three cars bought in Egypt is sold by our company.

Our position of dominance was further underpinned when we were given the master franchise for GM parts, selling on parts to other dealers. There was one final step we wanted to take in cementing our long-term relationship with GM. GM's multi-dealer strategy was designed to mitigate the risk of a monopoly provider going bust. But we thought we could work even better together if our interests became fully aligned. It was not an easy decision, and my brothers and I debated it often, but we eventually agreed to offer GM equity in our business and a seat on the board. That way they could see how the business was performing. GM did its due diligence, taking 10%, and continues to remain as a shareholder to this day.

There was one final legacy of our original agreement with GM that we wanted to address. GM's wish for us to operate three separate businesses, under the umbrella of a holding company, meant we had four legal departments, four finance departments as well as competing sales and marketing teams across the companies. After merging the three automotive dealerships in 2001, we became Egypt's largest GM dealer under the brand of Al Mansour Automotive, which remains our name to this day. It had been a gradual 25-year process but by the early 2000s, the structure and the market power that I craved were finally in place.

• • •

When distributorships in other territories became available, GM began to ask if we would be interested in taking those on as well. So, we went on to become GM's exclusive dealer-partner in Iraq, Libya, Uganda, Ghana and elsewhere in west and south-east Africa. We also have continued to invest in that business, which has grown strongly and become extremely profitable over the decades.

When GM sold Opel to Stellantis, the owner of Peugeot, in 2017, it gave its approval to us remaining in our current position under the new ownership. Stellantis later switched its Peugeot dealership to us too, so today in Egypt we are now the exclusive distributor of Chevrolet, Opel and Peugeot vehicles. We sell 8,000 vehicles a year for Opel and around 14,000 for Peugeot.

It has not been plain sailing. Another fall in the value of the Egyptian pound in 2016 caused new pressures as car sales suffered. We had to inject more capital into the factory, raising our share of GM Egypt, the entity in control of the facility, to 26% from 21%. Some advisers said that automotive dealerships were in decline elsewhere and online sales would eventually overtake brick-and-mortar operations like ours. But this company was our heritage, and it was my father's legacy. We needed to develop a new strategy, rather than give up and walk away.

Many of our biggest customers over the years have been corporate clients buying fleets of GM trucks and other vehicles for their employees. GM remains the bedrock of our business. But our new strategy has focused much more on the family car, provided by other manufacturers. I think this diversification strategy has been one of our best moves since the company was founded.

The dominant players in the global automotive sector have changed over the years. They used to be the large American brands, such as GM and Ford. Then European brands increased their global reach. Volkswagen (VW) was at one stage the world's largest car manufacturer. Fiat merged with Chrysler, and Daimler and BMW gained more control of the market for executive vehicles. We have been through the era of the 'Japanese invasion', with Honda and Nissan becoming major players in America and Europe. Toyota has taken over from VW as the world's biggest volume car producer, while South Korea has made sizeable inroads through Hyundai and Kia. Now I believe that the pendulum is swinging towards China because it still benefits from relatively low-cost production as well as enormous economies of scale. I went to China in January 2019, and signed an agreement with SAIC Motor Corporation, the state-owned Chinese company that is a long-term partner of GM and has become the nation's largest automotive manufacturer and a rapidly emerging force in the global motor industry.

Since 2011, Shanghai-based SAIC has owned the famous MG brand, which was founded as a manufacturer of the sports car in England in the 1920s. We visited the business and told the management that the brand has great potential in Egypt, where it is well-known and benefits from its rich heritage. We agreed to become SAIC's dealer in Egypt, selling 4,000 vehicles in our first year and around double that figure in the following year. Our MG operations in Egypt tripled production volumes in 2018–21 to become one of the top sellers of passenger cars in the country, selling more than 20,000 MGs in 2021. We are also now SAIC's dealer in sub-Saharan Africa. So, we have expanded our footprint from commercial vehicles, such as pick-ups and 5-ton trucks, to family cars and SUVs and invested heavily in marketing, training and quality of service. We are now preparing to produce MG cars from our Cairo factory in addition to GM saloon cars and 4.5-ton trucks. We still operate the master franchisee for GM in Egypt, with nobody able to sell a new GM car in Egypt without our approval.

The same is now also true for Peugeot, Opel and MG in Egypt, and all the other countries where we have distributorships. Our sales volume in our territories increased by 100% in 2019–21, despite the Covid-19 pandemic. I also like to believe that Mansour Automotive gave a major boost to Egypt as it opened the market up to the West. General Motors now ranks alongside other success stories such as Coca-Cola, which have made the USA the nation's leading foreign investor and most important trading partner.

It has been quite a journey. We have estimated through our calculations that there has been a total return since 1975 of about 17,000 times our money. Put another way, for every dollar we have invested in the business, we have got back $17,000. That is a remarkable testament to the hard work and dedication of so many people and the legacy of my father.

However, the journey is far from over for Mansour Automotive. Education is part of this. Egypt has seen a steady decline in road accidents over the past years that parallels with national efforts to improve the countrywide road network, but there is still much more to do. We have run a number of road-safety campaigns over the years and will not let up until the number of accidents and deaths on Egypt's roads decreases substantially. One area where we will continue to focus is in educating people on the benefits of wearing seat belts which, although a legal requirement in the country, is still seen by many motorists as an 'option'.

As I think back on where I have lived and what happened, I can see Egypt was a more difficult place to navigate and prosper when I was young. The road linking Alexandria with Cairo is only about 130 miles (220km) long, but as a child it felt as if we were crossing the Atlantic. Today, it takes only about two and a half hours to drive, but back in the 1950s, when the road was narrower and cars were slower, the journey took much longer. My parents and their staff would meticulously plan the journey for days, even weeks. From sandstorms to dangerous drivers, there were various risks to manage. There was the time when it was only thanks to the quick thinking of my travelling companion that we stayed on the road after our driver fell asleep at the wheel. My companion managed to grab the steering wheel before we were flipped over, possibly saving our lives in the process. My sister and her husband were fortunate to survive a very bad accident on the same stretch of road in the 1970s after a tyre blew, sending their car spinning into the path of an oncoming vehicle. It also was not a road you ever wanted to break down on.

We also want to help to spearhead the country's push into electric vehicles. In December 2021, in the presence of Egyptian prime minister Mostafa Madbouly, we agreed to explore the potential for the joint manufacturing of electric cars in Egypt. Mansour Automotive is assessing the production requirements and estimated volumes that we would need to make a success of electric-vehicle manufacturing, as well as the degree of incentives that would be necessary from the government. In 2022, two GM executives and I met President Abdel Fattah El Sisi as part of the preparations for the 2022 United Nations Climate Change Conference, more commonly referred to as COP27, held in Sharm El Sheikh, Egypt. We sponsored COP27 in partnership with GM and supplied a fleet of 150 electric vehicles to the conference to transport heads of state and other dignitaries to the venue. This meant a huge amount to me personally. Egypt faces many climate vulnerabilities, and I am determined that we will play our part in the path to net zero.

My ambition is for Mansour Automotive to pioneer EVs in the region. The idea is to use Egypt as an export hub to take electric vehicles into Africa. Egypt's government is being highly supportive, as the country's automotive manufacturing, sub-assembly and components sectors are key parts of President El Sisi's integrated industrial strategy.

The car industry is clearly poised for an exciting new era: another industrial revolution with an emphasis on advanced technology and smart production. As I was writing this book, the government of Egypt once again imposed restrictions on vehicle imports, as it had done in the 1980s, amid a foreign exchange crisis. But our business has never been more resilient than it is today, with a diversified product line and capacity to increase production. We have overcome challenges before and will do so again, ensuring that Mansour Automotive remains at the forefront of the sector's continued innovation.

CHAPTER SIX

Family ties

I dearly wanted to marry and start a family, and shortly after turning 30, I met the right woman with whom I would go on to build this life. Aged 18, Awatef Hassan – known to her family and friends as Fafy – came from a well-known family in Egypt. Her father, Mansour Hassan, a cosmetics exporter and manufacturer educated at the University of Michigan, had served in Sadat's cabinet. Fafy and I met at a wedding in 1978 that she was attending with her friend, Amina Mansour, a cousin of mine. I later discovered that her brother, also called Mohamed Mansour, had struck up a friendship with my younger brother Yasseen at George Washington University in Washington, DC, where they were both undergraduates. *Piccolo mondo* as the Italians say.

As we were introduced, I was immediately drawn to her. And only after the second time meeting her, I decided to approach her father and seek his approval to court her. Much to my relief, he was immediately supportive, letting me know that Fafy was soon to travel to America to visit her brother in Washington, and that he would be happy for me to meet her there.

I was already due to fly to Rio de Janeiro on an Air France Concorde from Paris to attend the Brazilian Grand Prix, and from there I would fly on to Washington, DC to meet Fafy. As someone who had studied aeronautical engineering and had always been fascinated by the technology of flight, I could not have been more excited to be flying to Rio by Concorde. I remember sitting next to a guy on the plane who was attracting a lot of attention from the cabin crew and other passengers. When we stopped in Dakar, Senegal, to refuel and disembarked, the passenger next to me was greeted by a pool of reporters and photographers. I knew he must be somebody important so after some time I asked him whether he was travelling to Brazil for business or pleasure. He replied 'pleasure', but it was obvious he didn't want a conversation. I asked him what he did. He looked at me almost with disgust, as if his pride was deeply hurt, and replied, 'You really don't who I am, do you? I'm in the entertainment business.' I said, 'Really?' About half an hour later I tried again. 'What type of entertainment?' He said, 'Well ... guitars, music.' I said: 'Oh really, I like music.' The day after we landed, I saw a photo of the guy arriving at the airport on the front page of the local newspaper. The story reported that the man in the photo, George Harrison, the ex-guitarist for the Beatles, was attending the Grand Prix. *Oh my God!* I thought to myself. Even though I'd been a fan of the Beatles, he had aged and I really had no idea it was him!

Once I reached the USA, Yasseen, Mohamed, Fafy and I spent several weeks together in the capital, and it was one of the happiest periods of my life. Free from chaperones, we explored the city, met for lunches and dinners, and as Fafy was a keen ballerina, went to performances together. It was romantic and exciting. Fafy coined a name for me, 'Misho', which she and my close family still call me today.

I was not yet wealthy and had used my savings to purchase a gift from a store in DC that I was certain would impress Fafy and would sweep her off her feet. It was a diamond-encrusted Van Cleef watch and cost around $5,000, equivalent to roughly $20,000 nowadays. I put the box in the glove compartment of my rental car and picked her up for lunch from her brother's dorm where she was staying. She took out the box, opened it, looked at the watch and said, in a matter-of-fact way: 'Thank you very much', and closed it again. I was a little disappointed with the understated response, but I had learned something new and endearing about her. This was who she was. Collecting material possessions is not important to her. She did wear the watch for years, and she was touched by any gift, regardless of its value. For her, the thought and gesture was always far more valued. I joked that once we had kids, I'd buy her a bag to carry diapers and other essentials for the baby, and she seemed far more excited about that. She had faced tragedy as a girl and understood what was important in life. Her mother, Suzanne, died tragically young at the age of 37 from cancer, enduring immense pain for three years before passing away in 1976, when Fafy was just 16.

By the end of our month spent together in DC I knew that I was in love, and when we returned to Egypt, I proposed and we organised an engagement party. We married in Cairo on 4 October

1979. The witnesses at my wedding were President Sadat and Vice President Hosni Mubarak (who would go on to succeed Sadat two years later, following the president's assassination). Our wedding reception, which was celebrated with over 1,000 guests, was hosted at Mena House, the legendary hotel close to the Pyramids where Roosevelt and Churchill met in late 1943 to discuss their plans for D-Day and the liberation of Nazi-occupied Europe.

In 1980, we had our first child, Mansour, named after my father-in-law. The day of his birth, 28 June 1980, was the happiest of my life. I gave our employees a bonus of one month's salary to mark the occasion. A joke doing the rounds in the company was that the workers hoped I'd next become a father of twins so that they could secure a bonus worth two months' salary. As it turned out, two years later I had another son, Loutfy, named of course after my late father. He is my rock and a worthy carrier of my father's name.

Mansour and Loutfy are the dearest things in my life. I always say that the love for one's own child is the highest blessing. They had a lovely childhood, and I adore being their father. Mansour has always been funny, charming, and could be quite mischievous but always lovable and is great company. He is happiest when he is at home in London, reading books and spending time with his soulmate, Natalya, whom he married in 2012. He is my eldest son and our bond is unbreakable. Loutfy has a great heart, a brilliant mind and has never given me a day of worry. His humility is one of his greatest facets and he is a natural leader and someone who thrives on responsibility. Loutfy is devoted to his family. He and his wife, Mai, are amazing parents to their four beautiful children-Mohamed, named after me (who also goes by the nickname of 'Misho'), Omar (known as 'Rico'), named after Mai's father, Jaida, who was born in 2021, and Kaila, who was born in 2022.

As Mansour and Loutfy grew into adolescence, Fafy returned to her passion for ballet, which she trained in as a child. As a result of an injury she sustained in 1992, which damaged her neck while training, she was diagnosed with the debilitating condition fibromyalgia that caused her dancing to stop. She has gone on to endure over thirty years of pain and fatigue, and it has been devastating for her, and despairing for my sons and me to see her go through it. We have visited and consulted with doctors around the world, but the search for a treatment to alleviate her suffering continues.

Although severely restricted with dancing, she was able to continue with her art. She likes to paint the 'real' Egypt – people sitting in cafés, the bustle of the bazaar. She has even painted some portraits of me, which I love. Conscious that some people might choose to buy her work because of her married name, she always signs her paintings Awatef Hassan. A measure of her talent came in 1996, when she showed around seventy of her paintings at a concert to mark the opening of a library in Cairo, hosted by the wife of the then-president Mubarak. The paintings sold out in less than an hour, raising around E£150,000 for the Children's Cancer Hospital in Cairo.

Before the fibromyalgia developed, she would take a much more active interest in my work and the business. She always has an instinct for what may be around the corner, a sixth sense almost, for what risks or opportunities may arise. If she was uncertain about a course of action, I would always listen thoughtfully and take great interest in her advice. I have always deeply trusted and followed her instincts.

•••

On 6 October 1981, we were all rocked by the assassination of President Sadat during a military parade in Cairo to celebrate the eighth anniversary of Egypt's crossing of the Suez Canal during the Yom Kippur War. A group of terrorists sprayed bullets into the president and others in the stands, killing him and ten others and wounding a further 28 people including Mr Mubarak, who was hit in the hand. Governments across the Islamic world that had opposed the Israel peace agreement welcomed the killing. We were horrified but also relieved that Fafy's father, Mansour Hassan, had a narrow escape. If the attack had been only a few weeks earlier, when he was still the spokesman of the National Democratic Party and a senior minister, he would have been sitting close to the president during the ill-fated parade. But he had withdrawn support for Mr Sadat over the president's authoritarian decisions after the peace agreements, which had stirred up a lot of tensions inside Egypt, and had been discharged from his ministerial duties. The president was also said to have been alarmed by a Lebanese magazine captioning a photograph of Mr Hassan as 'Egypt's next man', as well as the increasing political leverage of his former protégé. Nevertheless, I believe that Sadat loved my father-in-law and would have brought him back at some stage had he survived the 1981 attack. Mansour Hassan returned to serve as the chairman of the Advisory Council of Egypt in the transition period of the Egyptian revolution in 2011. He announced in March 2012 that he would run for president, but died later that year at the age of 75.

CHAPTER SEVEN

The Caterpillar that refused to crawl

There is a wise old saying that when you are in a hole, stop digging. We seemed to take the opposite advice as we moved from cars to excavators, and when we saw a hole we told everyone to keep on digging. Churchill's 'Dig for Victory' slogan during World War II (a government initiative directing people to grow their own food during the war) seemed apt. Digging was a transformative way forward for us, alongside cars, and it took us on a completely new adventure.

This new direction came about in 1977 when we won a contract with Caterpillar, the American company that constitutes the world's leading manufacturer of construction and mining equipment, off-highway diesel and natural gas engines, industrial gas turbines and diesel-electric locomotives. During the initial period of Anwar Sadat's presidency, Egypt remained a largely socialist country with most industry and trade still owned by the government. However, Sadat wanted to encourage a private sector and grow the economy. With its core business key to large infrastructure projects, Caterpillar saw the potential and wanted to enter the Egyptian market. The nation's ambitious pipeline of building roads, energy development and housing and commercial construction would need thousands of bulldozers, reloaders, excavators, scrapers, off-highway trucks and generators. Illinois-based Caterpillar wanted to be the company that supplied them.

Entering the market would not have been an easy decision for the company at a time when it was far from the giant that it is today. Caterpillar's revenue in 1977 was below $6 billion, compared to $59.4 billion in 2022, while the group's stock market capitalisation was a mere fraction of its peak value of $131 billion reached in May 2021. Egypt was deeply foreign territory to the Midwest US company and its first requirement was to find someone who could be trusted to run its modern dealership there. Management asked around and Citibank recommended three young men from an Egyptian family who were making a success out of selling cars for General Motors. Caterpillar approached us, and we met their team.

Caterpillar we learned is a traditional company that likes to forge deep relationships and stay loyal to its chosen partners. It is part of its make-up to place a high value on personal trust and respect. Presumably, for the group, we seemed a perfect fit; US-educated, reputable, ambitious and familiar with the American way of doing business.

After some initial meetings, we were selected to become the Caterpillar servicing dealer in Egypt. Youssef was our contact for

Caterpillar. As with the automotive company, my siblings and I founded the business with only a modest amount of start-up capital and, once again, our properties and other personal assets were put up as collateral to secure the line of credit that we needed to be able to import the machines from the US.

The next step was to find a name for our new Egypt-based Caterpillar dealership. Mantrac, an abbreviation of the first letters of 'Mansour' and 'tractor', fitted the bill and so began a long and lucrative partnership. Taking on the Egyptian dealership for Caterpillar was a landmark decision that has helped our group to grow and prosper.

We selected an executive team from Caterpillar's own operation to come to Egypt, including Barry Klink, who was appointed Mantrac's first CEO, as well as Steve Butler, John Cerkvenick and James Pringle, among others, who collectively managed the business from 1977–1982 while Youssef managed the automotive dealership in Alexandria. The Americans' task was to help us establish positions in Egypt's oil, gas, power generation and construction sectors. Founded on some land on the outskirts of Alexandria, Mantrac was the first company in Egypt to specialise in construction equipment and generators as the authorised servicing dealer of Caterpillar products. Our internal speciality was marketing and branding while the former Caterpillar team did much of the heavy lifting. The strategy was to position the Caterpillar brand at the forefront of Egyptian infrastructure that would need modern construction equipment. We knew that it was a medium- to long-term play but there was a great deal to go for, as the national economy revived. The expat team from

America laid good foundations, winning orders from a range of lucrative clients.

We learned from some mistakes we made during the establishment of our first automotive business. Although Mantrac borrowed capital in Egyptian currency to fund investment in Caterpillar equipment, when Egypt's currency was devalued in 1978 as the nation abandoned its two-tier exchange rate, Mantrac was stable because its security against its loans had been deposited in dollars. After Hosni Mubarak took over as Egypt's president in 1981, increased government spending on infrastructure led to many other orders. By 1982, Egypt's GDP had grown to $27.6 billion, from only $14.4 billion in our first year of operation. The boom had officially begun.

Despite the home-grown nature of the ownership, however, Mantrac was perceived in Egypt as an American company and by 1982, the time had come to remove the proverbial training wheels and ride out on our own. The expat team had done very well and established a succession plan, which made it easier to transition to a mostly Egyptian leadership group that at the time included Onsi Nagi, Osama Wafa and Hany Elkoly. During this time I remained largely focused on the automotive business.

Then, in 1992 we took another expansionist leap of faith. Philip Morris, another American conglomerate, approached Youssef with a plan for us to become its distributor for Egypt. The agreement was reached, and Youssef stepped down as Chairman at Mantrac to oversee the distribution business while I switched to heading up Mantrac.

I have been immensely proud to witness the extent to which

the Caterpillar equipment that our company supplied has transformed the nation of Egypt. Every project we support is important and worthwhile, but I've highlighted just a few of those that have come to mean a lot to me. The pace of population growth and infrastructure development in Egypt over the last 40 years has been rapid. For example, we have supplied equipment for the construction of the equivalent of 22 major cities.

One project alone had the ambitious aim of complementing Egypt's famous Nile Valley with the construction of the New Valley Project, a system of canals in the south of Egypt to carry water from Lake Nasser to irrigate part of Egypt's Western Desert, which in turn forms part of the Sahara. As part of this huge infrastructure development, there was a commitment to reclaim 500,000 acres of land by planting it with strategic crops, including wheat. We started by supplying 120 machines for work beginning at a canal inlet 8km north of Toshka Bay, which has given the system its present name of the Toshka Canal. The canal was originally planned to stretch 310km. Fifteen years later it was still 60km short of its target but work on the remainder of the project was revived under the current president, Abdel El Sisi. The Toshka Project was credited with protecting Egypt from the danger of high floods in 2020 and 2021. It also protected Egypt from a doubling in the price of wheat due to the Russian invasion of Ukraine in 2022.

We supplied a fleet of machines for the New Suez Canal Project, which made it possible for ships to pass through the waterway more quickly. Over 400 items of our construction equipment, including more than 140 articulated dump trucks, were used on the Galala Plateau Project, which moved more than 125 million tons of limestone to construct the El Galala, a new city complete with a university, resort and major roads network. In the new city of El Alamein, more than 600 of our machines were involved in the construction of what became one of the most important tourism development projects in Egypt.

Other projects include helping to revive 1.5 million acres of Egyptian countryside, assisting in the development of Egypt's high-speed electric railway and providing machinery to build Cairo's new monorail. In mining, our machines have excavated gold at Sukari, Egypt's first large-scale modern mine, and 238 million tons of black sand. There have been hundreds of kilometres of roads laid, gas and electric power projects and work on stadia when football's African Cup of Nations was hosted by Egypt in 2019.

By the time I took over Mantrac from Youssef, we had already carved out a strong market share in Egypt. However, there were worries for Caterpillar's distributors due to long-running industrial action in America. Members of the powerful United Auto Workers Union had gone on strike over pay and benefits. As the dispute dragged on, weeks turning into months, we became increasingly concerned about where we would get our products from. But Don Fites, the Caterpillar chairman, kept the plants running, many of his senior managers even joining the production lines to ensure that the machines were completed.

It was a time when others may have gone on the defensive, but I wanted to expand internationally. I travelled to the company headquarters in 1995 and had to pass noisy, can-rattling picket lines to gain access to the executive offices. Bodyguards accompanied us to the chairman's seventh-floor office. It may have seemed as if Caterpillar was under siege, but I went there determined to look outward, not inward. I wanted to secure Don's support for our plans. I explained that Mantrac had a strong balance sheet and that we wanted Caterpillar dealerships in other territories. It was unusual for an Egyptian company to be espousing global expansion but I told the chief executive that if we could not expand, we would want to invest our money into Caterpillar itself. 'Yellow is all we have,' I said, referring to the group's corporate colour.

These kinds of discussions are rarely resolved quickly. But we had put down a marker. And so it was that the following year, in 1996, I finally received the call that I had waited so long for. It was a district manager at Caterpillar, and he had news of an opportunity in sub-Saharan Africa. When I asked him where this would be he replied, 'Nigeria, Ghana, Sierra Leone, Kenya, Tanzania and Uganda.'

I was excited, and a little surprised. I knew that those six African territories were operated by Unilever, the Anglo-Dutch company best known for Lipton Tea and Dove soap. Unilever had been trading in Africa for decades. It transpired that its board had decided to exit non-core businesses, which it judged included its Caterpillar dealerships in the east and west of the continent, which were mostly run from Unilever's UK premises in Berkshire, England. 'Would you be interested?' he asked. I didn't hesitate – my immediate answer was 'Yes.'

Not everyone was convinced that it would be the right move.

Mergers and acquisitions are always risky but I knew this was the opportunity we had craved, and this would be our first merger. However, Unilever's African service territories were relatively unknown quantities and I was constantly met with discussions that ultimately said, 'we know nothing about sub-Saharan Africa.' One vice president said to me, 'I have never even been to Nigeria. Why would we go there? It is a big unknown for us where we might lose money there.'

Despite this, Mantrac Egypt was already successful and we led the domestic market. I knew that if we wanted to increase our growth we would have to expand internationally. An opportunity like this may never come along again. 'We are going to do it,' I replied.

The potential was clear. Nigeria had the biggest economy of the six territories on offer, with a GDP of $54.4 billion – although smaller than Egypt's (then $63.6 billion) and a fraction of the size of South Africa's economy ($147 billion). The value of the Kenyan economy was $12.1 billion, while Ghana's was $6.89 billion; Tanzania's was $6.5 billion; Uganda's was $6 billion; and Sierra Leone's was $850 million. We were betting that those numbers would grow significantly.

First though, we had to surmount the challenge of tough negotiations with Unilever. The Anglo-Dutch group hired Goldman Sachs to negotiate the disposal, while we were advised by Deloitte & Touche. Unilever, which planned to sell a UK Caterpillar franchise to Canada's Finning, a large group of Caterpillar dealers, already had a multinational lined up as a buyer for its

African territories and was sceptical of our credentials. 'Who are these Egyptians?' they asked. However, Caterpillar recognized Mantrac's past success and saw the significant potential we could offer in these service territories.

We visited the Unilever offices in London in 1996 for a difficult set of talks. Unilever had not wanted to sell to us, and we found them to be patronising at times. They tried to play hardball. We put together a multidisciplinary negotiating team, taking about 14 Mantrac executives to bargain directly with them. It was a very complex transaction that involved negotiating with a large corporation supported by a set of world-class advisers, acquiring seven different legal entities with all related issues including commercial, legal, labour, pension, tax and customer agreements.

It took more than a year of talks, but finally in 1997, we agreed to pay $60 million for the business. It was the first takeover of my career and I felt great satisfaction, and relief. Our cross-border expansion, which we had talked about for so long, could finally begin.

I went to inspect our purchase and found that some senior Unilever executives in Africa had lived in the most sumptuous villas. These acres of land and properties were company assets, so I knew that we had secured a good deal. Even on their own, the properties in central Nairobi, Lagos and Accra, and the housing for the expats that lived there – beautiful villas with landscaped gardens – were worth a great deal. I visited the main base in England to reassure the people there that they had made the right decision in remaining with the company.

The British employees may have been asking who this Egyptian company was, and whether we would spin off the business or cut the workforce, but my message was that we wanted to expand and hoped they would grow with us. I needed brilliant management talent, and I found it. When we were still negotiating with Unilever, I got to know a young man in the Mantrac sales team called Omar El Bakary who I noticed never seemed to go out with the others for dinner in the evenings and often would arrive the next morning with a spreadsheet and a set of recommendations. Omar always had a plan, so when we bought the business, we made him managing director of the business, which was called 'Unatrac.' When I later became Egypt's minister of transport, he served under me as my deputy minister, before taking up his post as chief operating officer of the combined Mantrac Group after I left office. He was one of my most loyal, trusted and productive lieutenants and he was a member of a group of people who were so instrumental in the growth and success of the business.

Omar, the rest of the team and I had a clear plan in terms of integrating the new businesses and overhauling the way they functioned. We felt there was enormous untapped potential. However, we needed to bring the Unatrac team along with us.

According to most studies, between 70 and 90% of acquisitions fail. The failure rate for cross-border takeovers is likely even higher. We were under no illusions about the scale of the challenge facing us. Not only did we have to continue serving customers and develop operations in six other countries, leaving the relative comfort zone of our home territory of Egypt to do so, but we would have to find solutions to integrate the people, management teams, systems and processes across borders. We knew we could accomplish it and Caterpillar matched our confidence, but to outsiders, the odds of success must have seemed startlingly small.

What we felt we needed to do to restructure and integrate the businesses could probably be accomplished in six months, but there would be no Big Bang approach. We took things slowly and steadily for the first 18 months, adopting a humble tone and a collaborative approach, involving and consulting the teams in the UK and Africa, always determined to bring them with us.

We did not want them to feel that this was an Egyptian takeover of a proud business. In 1997–2001, Unatrac remained separate to the Egyptian business and maintained some independence, with relatively limited involvement from Egypt. The message to the Unatrac team was essentially 'keep doing what you are doing, but we will support you with more talent, better processes and more investment into facilities, training and inventories.'

We empowered the local teams on the ground in Africa by devolving more responsibilities to those operations. For example, during the Unilever days, all sales and support functions were managed in the UK, but we wanted to change that so that the customers in Africa had local support, rather than counting on someone flying in from overseas.

We quickly realised that Mantrac had much better systems and processes than Unatrac. But we did not change much initially.

Slowly but surely, we began to show the Unatrac executives the benefit of what we had in Egypt and the value of adopting it at Unatrac. We brought the management team over to Egypt and were very accommodating. We took our time, we were very patient, because we knew if we rushed things, we could lose the support of the Unatrac people, and we needed them for the merger to be a success.

Gradually, the integration grew. Unatrac adopted more of our systems and processes, and during 1998 and 1999, we appointed approximately 10 to 15 executives from Mantrac Egypt into management roles within Unatrac. However, Unatrac remained largely a British business run by former Unilever executives by the end of the decade. The final step in the process, which in its way was as significant as the original acquisition, was combining Unatrac and Mantrac in 2001. After a gradual, four-year process of integration, this would enable us to do the restructuring that we felt was necessary to fully unlock value in the Unatrac side of the business. Omar, who had been on the Unatrac side, took over running the combined company, while the other heads of departments were split equally between Unatrac and Mantrac people. The combination created a melting pot of collaboration, creativity and innovation.

The transformation that has been completed since the early 2000s, bringing us right up to the present day, has been extraordinary. Over the last 15 years or so we have overhauled the management system, creating a matrix organisation with centralised department heads to oversee functions such as sales, marketing and finance. Most of the credit for this transformation is due to my son Loutfy, who took over as CEO in 2006 and has done a remarkable job in leading and taking the business forward.

Back in 1997, Mantrac Egypt's revenues exceeded those of Unatrac's, but today, the majority of our income comes from outside of Egypt, vindicating the decision to expand across borders to pursue long-term value and growth. We genuinely believe that the success we made of this merger was against the odds and could easily be a study case for business schools. For their part, managers at Caterpillar have told us they regard it as one of the most successful integration operations that there has ever been within the sector.

The new territories we added enabled us to continue to support the economic development of the continent. In Nigeria, our customers have included Dangote Industries, the country's largest conglomerate, as well as the oil group Shell and telecoms provider Airtel. In Kenya, our machines were used to build power plants for the nationalised power-generating company and for Kenya Breweries. In Sierra Leone our equipment was used in work with Africell, the nation's dominant telecoms company, and at the diamond mines of Koidu Holdings. In Liberia, Caterpillar equipment was sold to Sing Africa Plantation, the country's biggest logging company. In Ghana, Mantrac is supporting very large gold-mining operations with sophisticated service facilities. In 2019, it also inaugurated the Mohamed Mansour Component Repair Centre, the only accredited repair facility in Africa and the Middle East, which cost close to $60 million. Ghana is also a great example of Mantrac's commitment to skills and career development, having trained more than 500 young people since setting up a programme with mechanical engineering students from technical universities and institutions in 2016.

One day when I was visiting our Ghanaian operations, a young man working in the spare parts department named Edmund Martin-Lawson caught my attention. Soon after, he was managing the Nigerian Caterpillar business. It changed his life, he later told me, as for the first time he had his own house and car. He said I had asked everybody in the business to smile and that he was still smiling. Edmund is now head of two territories in West Africa for Mantrac.

If sub-Saharan Africa was a huge move, a potentially even greater challenge and opportunity was to follow. It was the late 1990s when we were offered an opportunity to establish a dealership in the oil and gas-rich territory of Western Siberia in Russia. The sheer scale of the terrain, its geology and its famously harsh weather were all areas where we had little or no experience. There were also huge geopolitical challenges and, not surprisingly, my management team was again highly sceptical. Russia's economy since the collapse of communism had been a shambles. Was it realistic that Russian companies at the time would be able to afford Caterpillar machines that cost up to $1 million apiece?

My view, however, was to think long term. 'Even if we lose money at first,' I said, 'this part of Russia has 30% of the world's oil and gas reserves. Its operators are buying Russian equipment for $10,000 apiece or cheap Chinese machines. Soon, they are going to value the efficiency of being able to use high-quality

Caterpillar equipment? My managers crunched some numbers and told me that we would lose $5 million every year for five years. 'Let's do it,' I said. 'I am banking on the future, 50 years from now. I am thinking for your children, for their children.' We went on to expand our operation in Russia through acquiring a dealer from Bergerat Monnoyeur, a French Caterpillar dealer. Of course, the Russian operations have more recently been heavily affected by the war in Ukraine. We suspended operations in 2023. This was a difficult decision, not because of the financial impact, but for what it means for the extraordinary men and women who have worked for us there. My first priority is always to our people and I didn't want to take any steps to wind down our operations until we could put a plan together to support them. Leadership means acting with a duty of care to your workers while at the same time responding to events.

There are always challenges in emerging and developing markets. In the early part of our time in Siberia, I was initially much more worried about the security. There were frequent kidnappings of Westerners, so I sent a man called Adel Selim, who was the Middle East and African taekwondo champion, to our office in Western Siberia. It was a no-man's land in the middle of the Ural Mountains and he was out there without a great deal of support, but he did a great job. Elsewhere in Mantrac's operations, we have had cases in Iraq of people being kidnapped. One was a very good lawyer friend called Sherif Elshayeb, who was chief counsel of our firm. He was going through a divorce and wanted to start a new life. A job was advertised and he applied.

'Why do you want to go to Iraq?' I asked. 'I just need to get out of here,' he replied.

Some months later I received a call from Iraq saying that Sherif's driver had gone to pick him up but found his house empty, with bloodstains in the bathroom and living room. Sherif was physically very strong and reminded us of Sylvester Stallone. He had heard noises in his villa in Baghdad and hid behind the shower curtain to try to evade masked kidnappers with machine guns. He was shot but survived. The men wrapped him in a sheet and slung him in the back of a pick-up truck before dropping him in the street outside a hospital. He crawled into the reception and asked one of the staff members to call me. I was completely shocked and had only one thought: *We must get him out.* 'Please, protect him. I will send a plane,' I told them. We never found out who the kidnappers were or what happened to them. Sherif survived and carried on working for us. When I became Egypt's minister for transport, I put Sherif in charge of parliamentary relations. He died peacefully at home in 2021. I owed him a great deal and promised him that I would pay for the education of his children and grandchildren.

Two other employees of ours in Iraq were kidnapped. I negotiated for two days, repeatedly telling the kidnappers that we would not pay anything, although my heart was bleeding for the victims and their families. Finally, we did get them out safely. It was wild and unsafe in Iraq, but we knew if we started paying ransoms it would never end. The tough approach paid off even though it was far from easy. The dominant thought in my mind was always about what it would be like for me personally if a member of my own family was subject to such a risk.

Countries with oil and gas reserves or gold and diamonds that require construction and power-generation equipment can be extremely difficult places in which to operate and Mantrac takes a safety-first approach in all situations. In Sierra Leone, during the civil war, there was one employee who kept living in our premises. He was sleeping there at night to protect the site, which was beyond loyal and another example of how much we owe our staff – something that never fails to move me. Regardless, I was always ready to jump in and start a new venture whenever a different territory opened. Only in Libya, where we worked with General Motors, did we close entirely when the civil war erupted. In 2020, we took on Ethiopia, a challenging country but one that has the potential for high growth in the years ahead.

In recent years we have integrated strategic planning as well as sales effectiveness functions and processes, developed world-class facilities and embarked on a digital transformation while building a diverse management team and workforce. Today, we are considered one of the leading Caterpillar servicing dealers in the world.

Mantrac has been an enormous success story in its territories, making a positive contribution to their economic and social development. As we celebrated the anniversary of the company's formation in 2022, we were able to look back on enormous progress not only for the business but for the communities it has helped to prosper. Our area of operation covers 8.2 million sq.km of land with a total population of 709 million and a total GDP of $1.8 trillion, while the workforce has grown to more than 3,000, which includes more than 850 service engineers. Our fleet of service vehicles across our territories now totals more than 400.

Possibly the number that I am most proud of, however, is the return that we have made on our initial, modest investment back in 1977. We calculate there has been a compounded annual growth rate of 27% on our initial paid-up capital, which equates to a total return since 1977 of about 20,000 times our money. Put another way, for every dollar we have invested, we have got back $20,000.

Despite the exponential growth that Mantrac has already achieved, we believe that this story is far from over and that the company still has a great deal more to offer. Egypt, still our largest market, had a GDP of $404 billion in 2021. According to credit ratings bureau Fitch, this is forecast to surge to $943 billion by 2030. Accountancy group PricewaterhouseCoopers has projected the Egyptian economy to reach a purchasing power parity (PPP) of a GDP of $4.3 trillion by 2050, by which time it expects Egypt to be the world's fifteenth largest economy. This would place it just behind Nigeria, where PwC sees GDP, calculated by PPP, also totalling $4.3 trillion by 2050 if it can diversify its economy away from oil and strengthen its institutions and infrastructure. Ghana's GDP of $77.5 billion in 2021 is forecast by the US Department of Africa to grow to $104 billion by 2030. With a recognised correlation between infrastructure investment and economic growth, we see continued success ahead but will retain the careful, prudent approach that has been the mainstay of our operations right from the beginning.

We have managed to compete in the hardest times, and I think we are now going to see the benefits of our investment as nations and economies grow. From a standing start in 1977, our Caterpillar business now has 12 dealerships and 61 branches in 12 territories, with offices in Africa, the Middle East and the UK. Mantrac operates one of the largest Caterpillar distributorship networks worldwide.

Urbanisation in Egypt has grown so much that our facility in Alexandria, which had been on the edge of the desert when we bought the land in 1977, is now generally regarded as being close to the centre of the city. The little road I drove along 45 years ago has mushroomed into a busy multi-lane highway teeming with cars, vans and trucks, many of which have been bought from our Mansour Automotive operations. It is almost impossible to put into words how proud I am personally to have been able to develop successful businesses in two different sectors, delivering astronomical returns on equity not once, but twice. With Man Capital, which I will discuss later, I hope to repeat the feat for a third time.

Whenever I visit Egypt, the extent of what we have created there moves me deeply. It is far greater than the bare facts and figures of our assets or even the number of jobs we have generated and supported there. It spans families and generations and has spawned marriages and children. At Mantrac's locations, I am surrounded by colleagues who have been in our business for 20, 30, 40 years. This is our legacy and I am committed to ensuring that it is passed on to the next generation in robust health. Caterpillar, which refused to advance at the sluggish pace of the insect that inspired its name, is still blazing a trail for us. Our family gave birth to this business and has nurtured it into adulthood with the same values that govern the rest of the group.

My great-grandfather, Deli
Fuad Pasha, was the hero of the
battle of Elena during the Russo
Turkish War. He went on to be an
influential figure, assuming a role
equivalent to Secretary of Defence
in the Ottoman Empire.

My parents were married in 1939,
just as the world plunged into a
global conflict. They could hear
the sound of artillery as the Allies
counter-attacked at El Alamein in
northern Egypt in 1942.

My father studied at Cambridge University in England in the 1930s. He went on to become one of the earliest Egyptians to graduate from the university.

My father worked tirelessly to grow the family business, which he founded in 1952 – only for his company to be confiscated by President Nasser's ultra-socialist regime in the mid-1960s.

My kindergarten class with our British teachers at Victoria College in Alexandria.
I am pictured on the back row, third from the left.

My father had an
amazing collection
of classic cars, such
as his Rolls Royce
(*top*). My brothers
Ismail, Youssef and
I got to explore one
while our father
and driver watch us
closely (*bottom*).

I was never happier than when my father took Ismail, Youssef and me to the beach in Alexandria.

This is one of only a few photographs of me in crutches, probably taken around 1962 during a vacation in Europe with my brother Youssef and cousin Soliman Mansour.

YOUSSEF L. MANSOUR

Youssef and I were siblings and fraternity brothers. Here we are in a yearbook for the FarmHouse Fraternity of NC State University, where we both studied during the 1960s. Courtesy FarmHouse Fraternity

MOHAMED L. MANSOUR

After I graduated and earned my MBA I returned to Egypt in the mid-1970s, roughly when this photo was taken. Those were my final years as a single man before I met my future wife, Fafy, in 1978.

My old fraternity brothers, James 'Bo' Boedicker (*left*) and Clyde Bogle (*right*) joined me at our old home on Chamberlain Street, Raleigh, during my visit to NC State University in 2022. Courtesy NC State University

The witnesses to my wedding to Fafy on 4 October 1979 were Egyptian President Anwar Sadat (middle) and Vice President Hosni Mubarak (left), pictured during the reception with Sadat's wife Jehan and my father-in-law, Mansour Hassan (right).

President Anwar Sadat of Egypt (left) and his wife Jehan (right) at my wedding to Fafy.

A framed copy of my marriage certificate is on display in my office.
The signatures of President Anwar Sadat and Vice President Hosni
Mubarak mean this has become an important historical document.

The day my elder son, Mansour, was born in 1980 was the happiest of my life. He lives a happy and private life with his soulmate, Natalya.

My younger son, Loutfy, is a worthy inheritor of my beloved late father's name.
He and his wife Mai are amazing parents to my four beautiful grandchildren.

My dear brother Yasseen, photographed with me in 2017 in France, has been such
an important part of my life. I am fortunate to have him as a brother and a friend.
Credit: Le Baoli, Cannes

I was always incredibly proud to serve my country. When this official photo was taken, I was the Minister of Transport for Egypt. I served from December 2005 to October 2009.

My darling mother was always calm and optimistic by nature. There is not a day that goes by when I do not think of her.

I have been made to feel very welcome in my adopted home of the UK. Here, Fafy and I had the great honour of meeting the then Prince of Wales, now King Charles III, at a reception.

Of all the politicians I have met, few were as charming as President Bill Clinton (*top*) whom Fafy and I met during a visit to Washington in the 2000s. His predecessor, President George HW Bush (bottom) was always gracious and generous and a person of integrity.

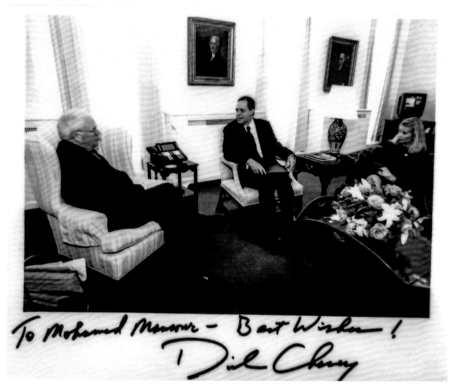

To Mohamed Mansour – Best Wishes !
Dick Cheney

Meeting then US Vice President and his daughter Liz in the White House was a great privilege. Liz Cheney, who went on to become a Congresswoman from 2017-2023, advised us on the establishment of the Lead Foundation in Egypt in the early 2000s.

Skiing has been one of our favourite pastimes as a family. Here I am during a trip with Fafy.

My darling sister, Rawya Mansour, has always put her brothers first. An early advocate for action on climate change, she has carved out a career in the field of sustainable agriculture.

My beloved siblings – Youssef, Rawya and Yasseen – are my rock and they have blessed me with many wonderful nieces and nephews.

I founded our family office, Man Capital LLP, in London in 2010. Establishing the firm after my time in politics was one of the best decisions of my career.

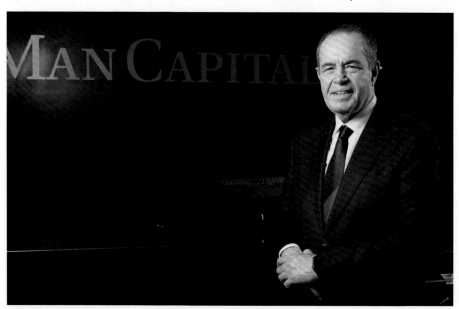

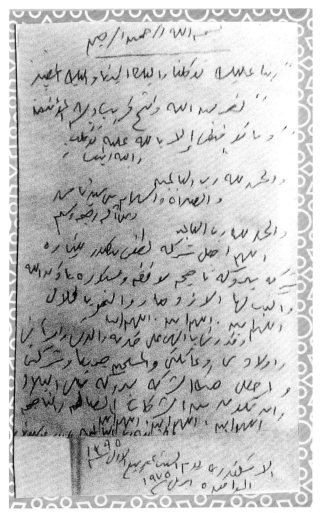

One of my most treasured possessions is a handwritten Arabic script written by my father in 1975 that we found inside the pages of his Quran after his passing. In the note, he pledges to serve his family and Egypt, do good through his cotton company and help the poor.

I am excited for a future in which electric vehicles – an example of which I showed to President El-Sisi in 2022 – will be increasingly important.

I was thrilled to deliver the keynote address to an audience of around 20,000 people at the Commencement Ceremony at North Carolina State University in May 2022, where I received an honorary doctorate. Courtesy NC State University

Rawya and I were delighted to be invited to join Prince Albert of Monaco's Planetary Health Pledge Club in 2022, which the Prince established in 2019 to promote sustainable development and the protection of the environment.

I was honoured to speak at COP27, the United Nations Climate Change Conference that was held in Sharm El-Sheikh, Egypt, in 2022. We discussed ocean finance and also I joined a roundtable with UN Secretary General Antonio Guterres on climate finance and vulnerable communities.

It was such a privilege to launch our new Major League Soccer club in San Diego in 2023. Joining me at the launch were (from left) my son Loutfy, Chairman Cody Martinez of the Sycuan tribe, MLS Commissioner Don Garber, investor group member Manny Machado of the San Diego Padres and Manny's wife, Yainee Alonso. Credit: San Diego MLS / Rick Romero

CHAPTER EIGHT

Big bets

There are, as we all know, seven ages of man, and T.E. Lawrence (AKA Lawrence of Arabia) wrote about them in his autobiography *Seven Pillars of Wisdom*. We have based our company's business ventures primarily on those seven pillars – the automotive sector, construction and mining equipment, the food service industry, tourism, retail, private equity and venture capital investing, and real estate. It is only a slight oversimplification to say they essentially cover cars, excavators, fast-food outlets, hotels, supermarkets, residential and commercial property developments, and investments in tech and other start-ups. We have a simple philosophy: our family will make every strategic decision with the aim of everyone prospering in the company. We do everything through very careful preparation and thought and then try to move with great speed and boldness.

Those pillars span every part of modern life. Under the Mansour reach, a total life can be constructed from the school you attend to the car you drive to the bulldozers making the roads and buildings in which you live or work, to the seed money for the creation of social media we all use and the food we buy in stores and eat in restaurants. Overarching all this is an investment vehicle, Man Capital, which looks widely at investing in everything from education to logistics.

Our operations span more than a hundred countries. Each of the pillars of our global conglomerate is run independently. Each brother is responsible for achieving objectives set out by the board. Youssef, Yasseen and I meet regularly to ensure that there is cohesion and harmony with our overall objectives. All major decisions must be agreed by the three of us. Each company within the group has a board that is chaired by either Youssef, Yasseen or me and comprises external directors as well as other family members. I chair Mansour Automotive, Mantrac Group, and Man Capital; Youssef chairs our distribution business, Mansour Distribution; while Yasseen chairs Manfoods, our McDonald's franchise, and Palm Hills Developments, a major real-estate developer. The chief executives report to the board and are often from outside the family.

I have never been a details man; my desk is normally empty. The only time that I had to be constantly on top of every detail was when I was a government minister. I quickly realised that I had to read everything and take great care over whatever I signed because the buck stopped with me.

In business, it is different. We have auditors, lawyers and other advisers; smart people who care greatly for the company's welfare. They protect the group. My job is to do the strategic thinking of what we will do next as well as what we need today. *Where should the Mansour Group be? Where should we be investing? What should we be pulling out of or backing away from?* These questions are in my thoughts daily.

I also try to have empathy with the people who work for us. You need to give people responsibility and judge them fairly on what they do with that. Somebody can be my friend, but if they do not perform, then I will want to know why. I naturally trust people and if they make an honest mistake, that is normal and fine. But if they keep repeating their mistakes and cannot see where they are going wrong then our business relationship simply is not working, and I have no problem with saying that we have to part ways.

I do not do the negotiating in meetings, I let other people do it. I do not talk too much. I prefer to listen, reflect and then decide. My strengths are more in forward planning and strategic thinking, taking our group forward, solving problems and trying to make things fair. It is also important to be humble. I question myself all the time. *Mohamed,* I think to myself, *have you changed? Have money and power altered the way that you behave?* If I think the answer is yes, I correct myself.

I do not want 'yes' people around me. I want people to tell me 'no' and explain why that is what they believe. When they do so, I listen intently. I like people who are probably more intelligent than I am who can help the business by telling it to me exactly as it is. Having more intelligent people working alongside me makes the company and myself act in a smarter way. When I am in meetings, most people say that I listen much more than I talk. I want to digest what I hear and spend my energy on decisions about the way forward.

Some of my best friends have worked in our businesses. I've mentioned Adel Khadr, who worked for Mansour Automotive for 46 years, and Omar El Bakary, who worked for Mantrac for 45 years. Many others are people I have known for many years. I know their families. They know me. I talk to many of them daily but I also delegate authority, giving complete autonomy and supporting them 100%. I don't want office politics in our businesses. There is a vision, a clearly communicated direction and a roadmap for getting from A to Z. And once that plan has been agreed upon by all of us, it must be delivered.

Technology, digitalisation, education and healthcare are our main predicted growth areas. There is an increasing involvement of venture capital, while the Mantrac construction equipment business is driven by major investments across the globe. That is how we strategise future development.

We always take great care and do our research – decisions to enter new territories and markets require detailed analysis to understand growth potential. My dream is for the Mansour name and brand to be truly global.

It was a significant moment for the Mansour Group when we became one of the first Egyptian companies to cross international borders with our Caterpillar distributorships in sub-Saharan Africa, bought in 1996. Our plan is to keep crossing continents and expanding, always investing for growth.

Our leadership style has developed differently from traditional Middle Eastern models. It is more like the Japanese philosophy of family. Our employees are treated as if they are part of our family structure. We focus on strategic thinking and big ideas. We keep our discipline tight and set ourselves a mission, with flexibility on how we can achieve it. Success is seldom an easy path and we do demand a certain level of work from our employees.

One of the quirks of our family is how my brothers and I have changed jobs and responsibilities within the group over the years. Like diplomats who are moved from different countries after a few years, it stops people getting stuck in a rut and forces fresh thinking and brings new perspectives. For quite a long time, I was only running our automotive business, but in the early 1990s, I moved to run the Caterpillar business. This created an opportunity for Yasseen to gain experience as a leader, and he did a superb job running the automotive business. Then we swapped so that we could avoid stagnation in our strategy and management style. Moving across the business is part of our strategic thinking. Sometimes, it can be easy to get too comfortable.

In the future, this is going to become more the responsibility of the younger generation in our family. Our children, nephews and nieces are mostly already spread throughout the businesses. Hopefully, they will be able to adapt with the times and prioritise the businesses, as we have always tried to do. We try to give them as much leeway as possible but always seek to ensure that they are operating in accordance with the core values the company was founded on.

Clearly, as the number of Mansour family members in our businesses increases, it may be harder to achieve consensus. In the past, it was just a case of securing agreement between the siblings. Now we have a lot more external input from people who may have a different view or agenda.

Around a decade or two ago, there was a fashion in the West for big businesses to focus on one area. Conglomerates were viewed as unwieldy jacks of all trades but masters of none; the benefits of diversification had been forgotten. Many publicly quoted companies in the West went on sprees of selling off so-called 'non-core businesses' and doubling up on one sector or operation where they saw the best growth opportunities. It is only comparatively recently that this has started to be seen as a great mistake. The British company GEC is a famous example of a business that fell victim to this new trend, recklessly abandoning the diverse range of aerospace, electrical and industrial businesses built up and run meticulously by its former chief executive Lord Weinstock for an ill-judged acquisition spree in telecoms equipment that saw it refocus and rebrand as Marconi before crashing the entire business ignominiously.

Most of my father's career was spent in the business of exporting cotton across the globe but his brainchild was to diversify the company's reach by investing in the automotive sector. We focused on our General Motors distributorships in Egypt after 1975, adding the Caterpillar distribution businesses two years later, which greatly helped add balance to our young group. When the Egyptian pound fell and our General Motors business was hit hard in the 1980s, the fact that Mantrac had debt in Egyptian pounds and assets in American dollars aided our overall corporate recovery.

More recently, as stock markets boomed after the financial crisis of 2008, there has been a trend for privately owned companies to go public. An excitable initial public offerings market, showcased by the successful flotations of the likes of Facebook and Airbnb, has fostered an obsession with publicly quoted companies. We are still frequently asked whether we have any plans for spin-off divisions, but as the Mansour Group is a family-owned collection of primarily private firms we have no current or planned intention to follow such prevailing trends that would narrow our business focus and find the company floating on one stock exchange or another. You can call us an unfashionable conglomerate if you like but we want our diverse businesses in the unconnected territories to be just as entrepreneurial, exciting and efficient as possible, while supporting them as they expand in size and magnitude to achieve constantly improving returns.

Over the years, the Mansour Group has built up a strong track record in finding and growing businesses. From General Motors' vehicles to Caterpillar's earth-moving equipment, from real estate to restaurants and from shopping malls to supermarkets, our group is now one of Egypt's largest companies. This all came about gradually. Globally, we employ more than 60,000 people across our businesses. We have 75 different nationalities who work together despite their different cultural and religious identities. It is all a long way from a simple Egyptian cotton business.

A liking for surprise and the unexpected has always kept us alert to new opportunities. When I moved to America and tasted a Big Mac for the first time, I never would have imagined that it would go on to be an important part of my financial future. But variety, as the saying goes, is the spice of life. As far as my business experience has taken me, single bets were not for me. I am a serial entrepreneur. I like to have more than one egg in our basket. I like big bets but for our company we seem to flourish best with new ventures and several strands to our rope.

It was Yasseen's idea in 1991 to approach McDonald's about opening its first restaurant in Egypt, only to be told that it was not looking to expand into the country at that time. But two years later the decision was overturned and McDonald's received 170 applications, and eventually granted two franchises in the country: one to us and one to another family.

Yasseen, who had been on the company's training course, opened our first Egyptian McDonald's restaurant in the affluent Mohandessin area of Giza in October 1994 – a year after McDonald's became the world's second most recognised brand.

It was no overnight success. We had to destroy early shipments of raw meat and sauces from Europe and Argentina when they failed Egypt's import rules. We struggled to find a local supply chain in Egypt for ingredients such as French fries, lettuce and buns. And only a tiny fraction of Egypt's population, which numbered 61 million at the time, had even heard of the Big Mac. Echoing what we had done with the Chevrolet brand, Yasseen's solution was to harness Egypt's great affection for football, signing a deal with Mahmoud El Khatib, Al Ahly's top scorer, for a TV advertising campaign. When the footballer endorsed McDonald's products in 1995, our market share took off like a rocket. We were also an early pioneer of McDelivery, making Egypt one of the first countries to have home delivery of McDonald's meals.

We expanded to ten restaurants and then bought another franchise, Orascom, which also possessed ten additional sites in its assets. Under Yasseen's chairmanship, Manfoods, the name we gave our McDonald's business, now owns and operates more than 150 McDonald's outlets, employing 5,000 people and serving an estimated 80,000 customers every day. It also supplies food to other McDonald's branches in the Middle East and Greece. Mohamed Ismail Mansour, the son of my late brother Ismail, is now chief executive of Manfoods, as well as running Infinity, a Man Capital-backed company focusing on renewable energy.

In addition to Manfoods, Yasseen focuses on MMID, which includes a wide portfolio: real estate, information technology, telecoms, tourism, media and entertainment. He is the driving force behind the growth of MMID's majority-owned Palm Hills Developments, Egypt's second largest real-estate developer, with 40 projects on 42 million sq.m of land. We own gated communities, hotels, business parks and even small cities. In 2008, Palm Hills became the only company within the Mansour

Group to be publicly listed, floating on the Egyptian Stock Exchange in Cairo.

Another pillar of the Mansour Group is Al Mansour Holding Company for Financial Investments (more commonly referred to as Mansour Distribution), run by Youssef. It is the largest distribution company in Egypt; we provide consumer goods to 130,000 outlets across Egypt, employing 8,000 people. Within Mansour Distribution are the supermarket brands of Kheir Zaman, offering food at affordable prices to customers on a lower income, and Metro and Fresh Food Market, which cater to more affluent customers. Combined, there are over 140 outlets in the portfolio.

Today the Mansour Group is as big in food as we are in transport. Youssef and Yasseen share my passion for empowering people and take pride in our companies' low staff turnover. We also always look out for each other.

My sister also plays her part with her individuality and talent. After studying commerce and law at Cairo University and decorative arts in England, Rawya married at 21 and has four daughters and a son. She set up an interior design company, RAMSCO Trade and Distribution, in the 1990s, which has been employed by the Egyptian Ministry of Foreign Affairs in Cairo as well as in the US and UK. She later moved into sustainable development and agriculture, designing waste systems for neighbourhoods, and recycling agricultural waste and re-cultivating vegetation in parts of the Egyptian desert. In 2019 she won the African Women Leadership Award, organised by *African Leadership Magazine*.

I always wanted my sister to have a job or interest in addition to taking care of her children. She was glad that I encouraged her talents in interior design and architecture. As a family, we are all slightly addicted to work but we know that family time is equally important.

Routine is key to my workday. I normally wake up quite early and begin to take calls with key managers from around 7.30am for three hours. Then I exercise in my gym, eat breakfast and go to the office around noon. I lead a well-organised life, but I cannot begin to keep on top of everything as we are now so large a business. I delegate as much as I can to people around me whom I trust completely.

I also spend a lot of time self-evaluating. When I am alone or driving somewhere, I reflect on my decisions, *Did I make the right call? Did I treat that person too harshly?* I am a thinker much more than a talker and am keen to learn from my mistakes. I tell this to my sons all the time. If you make a mistake, it is important to change course. I constantly question myself and my actions, but I never question our basic philosophy and its key tenets: quality of business, trust and growth. They never change, even though everything else does.

CHAPTER NINE

All roads lead to Cairo

Politicians' careers generally end in failure, or so the old saying goes. I don't know if my own experience proved that old dictum, but my time in politics certainly came to an abrupt halt.

My family has a long and proud history of serving Egypt and the Ottoman Empire. My great-grandfather, Deli Fuad Pasha, was an important figure in the Ottoman Empire's history. My father had served too, having represented the relatively poor Alexandria district of Karmouz in the Egyptian parliament for several years in the 1950s.

The events that led me to follow in my father's footsteps and pursue a career in politics began when I was in Paris in December 2005. I received a call from the office of the Egyptian prime minister Dr Ahmed Nazif, asking me to fly to Cairo to meet him. Nazif had been in office for 17 months, becoming Egypt's youngest serving prime minister since the founding of the Republic and the second youngest prime minister in the history of modern Egypt. Five days after his appointment, he had staffed his cabinet with 14 technocrats and well-educated neo-liberals. Nazif had entered politics through academia, previously being a professor in computer engineering at Cairo University. He established Egypt's national identity card project, created the country's first free internet connectivity plan, and increased public access to low-cost computing through the Egyptian Telecommunications Company. He was famous for stating in 2001 that 'outsourcing is nature's way of reversing the brain drain.'

I had met Nazif only once before and had been given little indication of what the meeting was about, but I knew that he wanted to reform the economy and guessed that he wanted me to join the government. Since the 1950s, most ministers had come from the ranks of academia, the military or the police. But I knew that Nazif wanted to bring in some experienced business leaders to open the country to foreign investment. 'Mohamed,' he told me, 'you're a proven business leader who is regarded in great respect in this nation. I want you to serve as minister of housing.' The prime minister explained that I would be one of several new appointees from the private sector to join the government on the same day.

The offer posed a dilemma. In Egypt, government ministers are all-powerful, a team of 30 individuals who essentially manage a nation of 100 million people. It is a great honour to be asked to serve and in Egypt, as elsewhere, there is a sense of duty to your country which means you accept such an offer. Such positions carry great prestige and a lot of people spend their whole lives striving to be appointed. I had engaged with government while serving for a period as president of the American Chamber of Commerce in Egypt, the most powerful business institution in Egypt. In this role I attended lunches with Egyptian government officials and was part of an annual delegation to Washington, DC. I was just not sure that I was best suited to the housing department and admitted to Nazif that I did not think I would be the right person for the position.

Two days later, I was asked to be the minister of transport. The housing role was awarded to my cousin Ahmed, who was moved from the tourism department, where he had served as a minister following his positions as chair of the Accor Group in Egypt, the owner of the Old Cataract Hotel. Of course, transport was closer to my area of expertise although motor vehicles and roads would be only a small part of my remit. On 28 December, I travelled to the president's office to be sworn in.

The other appointees included Zoheir Garrana, whose family operated in the tourism industry and who succeeded Ahmed as the new minister in the tourism ministry; Amin Abaza, who had experience of farming and was made minister for agriculture; the finance minister was Youssef Boutros-Ghali, the grandson of a former Egyptian prime minister and nephew of former United Nations secretary-general Boutros Boutros-Ghali; and Professor Dr Hatem Elgabaly, a leading healthcare entrepreneur who was appointed Minister of Health and Population. Rachid Mohamed Rachid had his position in the trade and industry ministry extended while Ahmed Ezz, a steel tycoon, was made chief whip.

In order to focus fully on the job, and also to remove any perceived conflicts of interest, I immediately stepped down from my outside commercial responsibilities. Youssef became chairman of Mansour Automotive and Yasseen replaced me as Mantrac's chairman, while Loutfy agreed to leave Goldman Sachs and head back to Cairo to learn the family business, starting off in Mantrac under Yasseen's mentorship. Goldman's then-chief executive Lloyd Blankfein later told me how impressed he was when he heard about the career sacrifice that Loutfy had made to support his family.

I also resigned from over 50 directorships including positions on the boards of Coca-Cola, Credit Agricole, the Cairo Stock Exchange and the American University in Cairo. The only exception was my chairmanship of the Lead Foundation, my not-for-profit lender, which was doing incredibly important work for underprivileged women and I wanted to continue to support it.

The next three and a half years were the hardest of my working life. I had been used to risking my own money. Now I was to be a steward of the nation's. There were 23 different authorities, employing 280,000 people. I would not be able to choose many of them or make many changes.

Once I was sworn in, the government gave me a car and a bodyguard and asked me to go straight to the ministry. It was a strange experience. Few people in the building knew who I was, and I did not know any of them. I was way out of my comfort zone. I needed a chief of staff and soon brought in my own team from Mantrac. I kept their work agreements intact to give them job security and allow me continuity.

My new mission was to upgrade Egypt's crumbling transport infrastructure but in all honesty, looking back, I really had very little idea of what I was getting involved in. Prior to my appointment, I had been involved in the establishment of Credit Agricole Egypt, a bank created after MMID and French banking group Credit Agricole acquired a majority stake in the privatised Egyptian America Bank. Egypt's socialist press, unhappy about the privatisation, denounced the takeover as being all about money and power. This was the tone of the media coverage as I arrived at the ministry. There would be no 'honeymoon' period.

Events unfolded rapidly as I accompanied Nazif to the World Economic Forum in Davos, Switzerland. My new status in government made it a very different visit from when I had previously attended the forum as a business leader. When you enter government as a minister, your life is no longer your own. Everything revolves around daily meetings with the prime minister. A kind of herd mentality develops. Everywhere the prime minister goes, he is followed by three or four government ministers, walking behind him. It did not seem real. People who knew me from previous experiences said: 'Mohamed, what's wrong with you?'

At Davos, I sat in on a session about what leaders should do in the first 100 days of a new role. It was a debate between some chief executives of major companies, including the boss of Vodafone. All the panellists advised against rushing to make any commitments, and counselled against speaking to the press too soon, which was particularly relevant for me because newspapers had already reacted badly to my appointment in the government. I thought I must be doing okay because I had been in the job for just over a month and had neither made any new commitments nor spoken to the press.

Eight days after Davos, I woke up on 3 February 2006 in my flat on the twenty-third floor of a skyscraper with a beautiful view of the citadel of Cairo, the Nile and the Pyramids. At about 11 o'clock, I went to my gym and while I was on my exercise bike, my mobile phone rang. It was a withheld number, so I immediately knew it must be someone in the government. On the other end of the line was my chief of staff, a former army colonel. 'Good morning,' he said. 'I hope you are well. Minister, a ferry left Saudi Arabia at seven o'clock last night and was supposed to have arrived early this morning. We think it has sunk.' As my feet turned the pedals of that exercise bicycle, my heart sank. I knew immediately that this was a terrible human tragedy. And it was on my watch.

I had been in the post for only a matter of weeks, and I faced my first crisis. I knew I had to be personally present in this tragedy. I would look after any of my employees who were caught up in a catastrophe. I had to be there for these countrymen. This was and still is my personal style but possibly it also betrayed a naivety and lack of political experience. I put on my suit, called Nazif, then spoke to the defence minister and the Egyptian army's commander-in-chief, Mohamed Hussein Tantawi, to arrange for a helicopter to take me to the scene of the disaster in the Red Sea. On the way to the heliport, I received a call from CNN, which already knew about the tragedy. A few days earlier, I had congratulated myself for not talking to the media. Now I had no choice. It was the first of dozens of media calls that came in from all over the world.

The ferry, the MS *al-Salam Boccaccio 98*, had been operated by a private Egyptian shipping firm called El Salam Maritime

Transport. It had been carrying about 1,400 passengers and crew. Most of the passengers were Egyptians working in Saudi Arabia and pilgrims returning home from the Hajj in Mecca.

The navy was scrambled, and I arrived at the scene, around 90km to the east of the ferry's destination of Safaga, as the sun was setting. When I flew over, the situation looked so bleak that I thought that we would do very well to save just 20 people. I could see all these people on the surface of what I knew to be a shark-infested sea in cold February temperatures. It was a horrifying sight. Out of hope as much as expectation, we sent fast ferries out to pick up any survivors. We were still bringing in people at about five o'clock the next morning. In the end, some 388 people were rescued but 1,031 people perished. It was one of Egypt's biggest peacetime maritime tragedies and gave me sleepless nights for a long time.

The catastrophe was not technically under my jurisdiction. As transport minister, I was responsible for the nation's ports and events up to 20km away from Egypt's sea frontiers. This tragedy was really a matter for the prime minister to lead. Yet, given the profile that I already had and the newness of my position, it was inevitable that I was going to become the face of this terrible accident in the Red Sea. These were dreadful times, and my heart went out to the families of those who died. Everything went into emergency mode.

Egypt's petroleum minister provided a robotic vehicle that could go 1km underneath the Red Sea to retrieve the computer data from the ship so that we could learn what had caused such a tragedy to happen. The operation made it into the *Guinness Book of Records* for being one of the deepest dives to retrieve a black box. The investigators discovered that a fire had broken out on the car deck around two hours into the 200km journey. The conclusion of the inquiry was that an accumulation of water used to douse the flames on the car deck had made the ship dangerously unsteady, and in rough seas the roll-on, roll-off vessel began to tilt. When a tipping point was reached, the ferry capsized and sank within minutes before an evacuation could be ordered. The captain lost his life in the tragedy.

Most politicians I talked to after this tragedy felt that I had made a mistake getting so personally and publicly involved. Had I been a seasoned politician, I would have perhaps managed events differently, staying put in Cairo and letting the government's minister of communication do the talking. But I am a human being, and if this had happened again, I would have done the same thing.

The crisis eventually abated, but the issues and the challenges did not. Running the ministry was going to be an enormous challenge. I realised very quickly this was going to be the hardest working period of my entire life. I was 57 years old and, although I had no way of knowing how long I would be doing this job for, I knew that it would be a relentless whirlwind of activity.

Transport felt like the most challenging of all government ministries. It included all the nation's highways and roads, which were mostly in poor condition and blighted by a terrible safety record; the nation's railway network, the second oldest in the world and in desperate need of modernisation; all the transport on the Nile; and all of Egypt's ports, which required upgrading and had received little or no foreign investment.

The rail infrastructure creaked and the rolling stock had not been upgraded for decades. The ministry had 700 locomotives that were supposed to be working but I discovered around half had been cannibalised for spare parts and were therefore useless. The rails and signals were in a poor state of repair and the punctuality and safety records were terrible. Egypt's railway system was heavily subsidised with ticket prices well below the cost of providing the service, which meant that the operation was losing about E£5 billion a year. Many of the network's 73,000 employees were underpaid and had not received adequate training from the state. I knew I had a huge challenge ahead. I also realised I had very few tools to implement meaningful improvements.

Everyone had an opinion about Egypt's transportation infrastructure – and mostly those views were negative. When a train was two hours late, I would get calls from the president. Whenever there was any news about Egypt's transportation network, whether good or bad news (it was usually bad), my picture was on the front page of various newspapers. There was one period of several weeks when I was only knocked off the front pages when Pope Benedict XVI said something that was interpreted as showing disrespect to Islam. A former admiral who was the head of one of our ports joked that I should convert to Christianity as a way of saying thanks to the pontiff.

We had personnel issues as well as infrastructure challenges. Many of the people working in the ministry had not been screened sufficiently, if at all – and our employees were underpaid. In a private family business, you might have known the people that work for you for many years. You select them, support them and they remain loyal to you. In politics, the civil servants are there when you arrive and they will still be there when you have gone. You have to work with whatever qualifications and quality they bring to the table. Morale was a big issue. I gathered around me a good team of young men and women from the Mansour Group, including my loyal friend Omar El Bakary, who stepped down as Mantrac's CEO and became my deputy minister. I found other talented people within the ministry and set about improving computer systems, merchandising and the way that the organisation looked after its staff.

I embarked on an ambitious plan delivering huge investment to revitalise the nation's economy. I took it upon myself to institute a period of reconstruction and reform and was backed by the prime minister to do so. Over the next four years, we built 20,000km of new roads and improved many of the existing highways. We contracted a French engineering company, Systra, to supervise construction of the third line on Cairo's Metro transit system, while plans for a fourth line were initiated and put in place.

A striking success was the Port of East Port Said, which was just a small operation when I took over the government position. We supported the Maersk shipping company to expand the container port there and, from a standing start, this very quickly became the third largest container port in the Mediterranean. It was soon dealing with 3 million containers per year and my objective was for it to overtake its Spanish and Italian rivals. We also upgraded the Port of Alexandria to meet global standards. My ministry also set about plans to build other container shipping terminals across the country. I saw no reason why Egypt could not have the biggest ports in the Mediterranean. The Suez Canal is naturally an extremely busy channel, with one-third of the world's container traffic reaching the Mediterranean via the canal, but it had not previously had the facilities or services to attract ships to dock. We attracted regular business from a French port line, and by 2008, the canal had delivered a 22% increase in its income over the previous year.

I wanted us to make more of the Nile, which was not being utilised properly as a transport and shipping network for the nation. I wanted the river to be used by boats and barges to transport cargo from the south of Egypt to the north and vice versa at lower costs, as happens in France with the Seine and Germany with the Rhine. Utilising rivers to move bulk commodities on barges is far cheaper than using roads so starting to do something there got our nation moving in the right direction.

By far our greatest challenge, however, remained Egypt's railroads, which were unsafe, due to many years of chronic under-investment and neglect. The accident rate on the rail network had been high for years and the quality and state of repair of the locomotives was terrible, with many of them a hotchpotch of parts from different manufacturers and eras. The system was unreliable and prone to frequent faults. Unsurprisingly, given all of this, the people operating and maintaining the trains and network, as well as providing Egypt's commuters and other passengers with something approaching a service, were disenchanted and unmotivated.

After learning that Egypt's railroad was the largest owner of land in the nation, owning thousands of acres around the railroad tracks, I reinvigorated the investment company within the ministry to utilise the real estate much better. We began upgrading stations, using the model of modern hubs with retail outlets that were prevalent in Europe. The historic main rail station in Cairo was given a major facelift. We upgraded the Alexandria–Bourg Al Arab railway line and provided the railway station and network in Alexandria with a commercial revenue. Tenders were issued for the commercialisation of concessions for stations in Alexandria, Cairo, Giza, Tanta, Luxor and Aswan. Egypt had not been using its railroads very much to move goods across the country. We started to remedy that, boosting income to the rail network. My aim was to bring it into profit so that it started to generate its own funds for investment.

We kick-started the development of land that was next to rail tracks, with shopping malls and consumer attractions also providing railroad revenues. Within my term of office, we stopped making annual losses of billions of Egyptian pounds on the rail network, achieving break-even and attracting private investors. Ashraf Rashed, the Egyptian ambassador to Italy, was extremely helpful, arranging for Egypt's railroad to be assisted by the Italian rail network, which sent eight senior rail advisers to help us with safety and signalling. We also launched an initiative to improve safety at open rail crossings. In total, we upgraded around 3,000 carriages and brought 200 new locomotives into service. Cairo's underground rail system received investment in a new line and Egypt's first ever air-conditioned carriages were provided on that new line.

I found the job so stressful because it was not my money that was at stake. When you are in business with your own money, you know you can lose a little or a lot but, ultimately, it is your decision. You control the risk and reward. In government, the funds at stake belong to your country and its citizens. This made me more emotionally affected by the ups and downs of political life.

Nobody wanted to pay higher rail fares or pay to use roads that they had always treated as free of charge. However, these changes were essential to bring investment into the transport network and begin to generate revenue. I realised then, if I did not know it already, that being a politician in the developing world is a thankless job.

However, ministerial stints in Egypt, like in most countries, rarely finish smoothly and, just as the beginning of my time in government was marked by a transport tragedy, the end of it was too. On 24 October 2009, a locomotive filled with passengers hit another train that had come to a stop after it hit a cow crossing the line near El Ayyat, 50km south of Cairo. The freak accident killed at least 50 people.

I travelled to the site of the crash to co-ordinate care for the injured and to see what had happened ahead of managing the government's response. I was accompanied by, Dr Elgabaly. The passengers who had lost their lives or were injured were our priority, and we did all that we could for them and their families. Egypt had benefitted from our investment programmes with a reduction in accidents since upgraded systems but the press coverage remained largely critical.

I believe that most fair-minded people in Egypt thought I had done a good job in difficult circumstances, beginning to remedy years of neglect and under-investment. We knew only too well that rail safety was a problem in Egypt. Deaths had fallen during my time in office – albeit from a very high level, with the peak being 2002 when close to 400 people had been killed in a single incident. But we knew that we had to do much more. Even the opposition party did not attack me over this crash or claim that it had resulted from any of my actions.

It was generally accepted that I had entered politics through a sense of honour and not because of any great ambitions. I had no interest in being prime minister or president. I knew in my heart that politics was not a career that I wanted over the long term. I am not built for it. When you are in government, you just have to do the best you can.

A big motivating factor in accepting the invitation to become a minister was because I knew that it would make my parents proud. My father, of course, did not live to see me serve in government. My mother, who was 82 when I was appointed, passed away at the age of 85 in 2008 after developing heart problems. The doctors in Egypt had told us there was not much that they could do, but we flew my mother to Hamburg, Germany, where a new approach to treatment was being developed to replace the aorta without anaesthesia. Many family members, including my siblings and cousins, travelled to Germany and stayed with her in that hospital for a month. Every cousin, child and grandchild was there. I would fly in to see her, spend a few days or a week with her and then fly out again. I told Egypt's president and prime minister that I was sorry, but my mother had to come first.

As she lay in that hospital, for the first time in her life she told us all what she really thought of us. She had always been so diplomatic but when she was not well, she really let everybody have it, telling us all our flaws. I was not spared her sharp comments – she told me that I could be arrogant and needed to come down a level or two. I had to take it on the chin.

She got through the operation but died a week later while she was recovering. We now laugh in our family about how forthright my mother became on her deathbed, but the criticism was well-meaning. Her true legacy will never be forgotten. On the day of her funeral service, the traffic in Cairo stopped, with thousands of people paying homage and respect to her. We returned her body to Alexandria for the burial.

In government there are factions and alliances and not everyone pulls in the same direction. During a debate in parliament, Mubarak's chief of staff argued that I was wasting money on advertising – I had fronted a TV campaign about the improved infrastructure – at a time when we were coming to terms with a tragedy on the railways. A colleague sitting next to me, who saw that I was annoyed by this, touched me on the arm and advised me to remain silent and not to use my ministerial right of reply. Even my political foes on the opposition benches defended me and said I had done my best. I sat silently and the next day the view in the cabinet was that I had dealt with the crisis well.

But the criticism from some quarters kept coming. I sometimes felt at a disadvantage with some of my peers who, as students, had been taught classical Arabic, the language of formality, elevated prose and elaborate oratory. My oratory style was more colloquial, which seemed to be a relative weakness. Some politicians may do very little of substance but are good talkers, and I learned that politics is as much about presentation and communication as delivery, possibly more so. I had never experienced people on your own side openly criticising and undermining each other. The opportunity to serve my country was a huge honour and very rewarding, but the politics that came with it made me feel uncomfortable. I was probably not thick-skinned enough for all the backstabbing. I knew there was so much that we needed to do to help the country and its people, and yet it seemed that some of my peers were more interested in scoring points against their real or perceived foes. It was exhausting, and I began to accept that I could not continue in the role for much longer myself. The time was approaching when I knew I would need to do the honourable thing and pass the baton to the next generation.

I felt at my lowest when one of the newspapers controlled by the government published a front-page headline about the rail crash that claimed 'Mansour is to blame'. I was in an impossible situation and knew that it was time to step down. I arranged a meeting with my wife and sons so that I could tell them that I was going to leave the government.

There was an old joke that no government minister had resigned since the time of Ramesses II, the third pharaoh of the country's nineteenth dynasty. You were either sacked or you died in your parliamentary seat. You had no autonomy – I had to ask for official permission each time I left the country. So, I knew it may not be straightforward to step down. I asked to be driven to the prime minister's office. Nazif seemed to know what was coming and one of his advisers tried to talk me out of it. But I was insistent: 'I have given nearly four years of my life,' I said, 'I have given the best that I can to the country and the ministry. I have done what I needed to do in this ministry. I think there is no more that I can do or give. I want to go now.'

Nazif said he needed to speak to the president, but I could not be dissuaded. They said they would let me go. And so, at noon, on 27 October 2009, I appeared on live television in Egypt, stating in a pre-prepared speech that I was resigning from my post. I was driven home where my wife, sons, brothers and cousin Ahmed were waiting. After having a light lunch togther, I packed two suitcases and left at six o'clock in the evening on a private plane to Paris to avoid being spotted on a commercial flight as I didn't want to get caught in a media circus.

I booked into a hotel in Paris and did my best to rest and recuperate. The next day I went for a walk along the Champs-Élysées and enjoyed a nice lunch, but I was in a daze. Everything was a blur. My phone would not stop ringing. Reporters wanted to know my reasons for leaving but I have a lot of businesses in Egypt and did not want to make any waves, so I remained quiet. My niece was getting married in Egypt the following day, but I told my sister I would be unable to make it. I turned off my phone for some respite after that. When I eventually switched it back on, my secretary called to tell me that Mubarak had been trying to reach me for two days, and had asked me to return his call. I called the president's office on the evening of 29 October, when his secretary answered and said: 'Yes, Mr Minister, we have been looking for you.' I was transferred to Murabak shortly thereafter.

I always knew what kind of mood Mubarak was in by how he addressed me. My father-in-law Mansour Hassan was a big competitor in Mubarak's eyes. Mansour Hassan was very open and democratic, but Mubarak didn't like him so the Mansour name was almost an insult to him. If he called me Mansour, I knew something was wrong. Whenever he called me Mohamed, I knew he was in a good mood. On this occasion his first words were, 'Hi, Mohamed. How are you?' So, I knew we were going to have a reasonable discussion. 'You know, you did the right thing,' he said. 'I didn't want you to leave but I know that you worked hard and did a good job. I understand.' We spoke frankly for close to an hour and I told him that he had to choose which path he wanted to take the country down. He always had insisted the country was free and democratic when everybody knew it was not. We talked about poverty in the country. Travelling round the country as a minister, I had met so many people in towns and villages who were struggling to make ends meet. 'There is a lot of dissatisfaction in Egypt and sooner or later it is going to bubble to the surface,' I warned him.

The following day Anas El Fiqqi, the information minister, called me and said he had been told what I had said to the president, and accused me of criticising his work. I explained that my view was that the president should reduce the government's control of the media, rather than pick and choose who was allowed to speak freely. 'This is my honest opinion,' I told him. 'It is not right and the reason I told the president what I did is to protect you guys, because sooner or later it is going to be your turn.' I did not know that revolution was coming, but when Mubarak fell 14 months later, El Fiqqi was placed under house arrest and later jailed, albeit subsequently acquitted.

After a week in Paris, Fafy, Yasseen and Loutfy joined me there. Then we all travelled to London, with Fafy and me staying in a hotel while Loutfy moved into our apartment in Kensington. Two weeks after my resignation, Nazif made a speech at the National Democratic Party's annual conference saying he wanted to thank 'the courageous minister Mohamed Mansour' for his 'exceptional work.' The prime minister went on to say that my resignation was 'a big loss' for Egypt. This part of the speech received a standing ovation.

I only talked to Mubarak on one further occasion, around six months later, in the spring of 2010 after he had a serious operation in Germany, making Nazif acting president for six weeks. I was in a meeting with a banker when my phone rang and it was the president's elder son, Alaa Mubarak. Alaa said the president had just returned home from his surgery and wanted to talk to me. 'Mohamed, I just want to tell you that you did a great job and that you did the right thing in resigning. You were always honest with me and very hard-working,' said the president. I was surprised that he had called but he stayed on the line for a ten-minute chat, at the end of which he asked me to let him know if I ever returned to Egypt. Later, I discovered that I was the first person the president called following his operation. Why he did, I will never know. I never saw or spoke to him again.

I knew from travelling around the country and region that major changes were brewing in the Arab world and that Egypt was likely to be impacted. One of the interesting aspects of ministerial life was travelling to meet world leaders, though these were not always enjoyable moments. In Tunisia and Libya, for example, I knew never to speak in my hotel room for fear it would be bugged. President Ben Ali of Tunisia was a particularly unpleasant dictator – even worse than Colonel Gaddafi of Libya. He was in charge of national security and believed that if you were strong enough to supress opposition, people would never successfully rise against you. Tunisia was a police state. So, as I watched television on 14 January 2011 as popular uprisings in Tunis forced Ben Ali to flee to Saudi Arabia after 24 years of oppressive rule, it was quite a moment. There was widespread relief that his time in power had ended. Ben Ali was stronger than any of his peer group of dictators, so when he fell, it was obvious that others would also topple soon.

It was clear that this wave of unrest and series of revolutions would engulf Egypt. I did not believe that Mubarak was a bad man. He was nowhere near as despotic as Ben Ali or Gaddafi. He was autocratic, not vicious. As a leader, he could be indecisive. He would defer decisions and say he wanted to think. I believe he had a good heart, but in the last years of his rule, I think he lost the will to govern. He could even be funny, joking with people to make them feel comfortable, but the people surrounding him were not the best. His son, Gamal Mubarak, who was practically running the country towards the end of his father's time in office, or certainly thought that he was, was very different; he lacked empathy and was quite cold. As the end for them neared, they became increasingly hard-line and resistant to change. But once their even harder-line leaders of neighbouring nations started to fall, there was little chance they would survive.

As the transport minister, I frequently toured the country's regions and villages and saw first hand the poverty and squalor that our people were living in. I would sit in village cafés, talking to local people and their unhappiness was evident. I remember addressing the American Chamber of Commerce in Egypt. I told the attendees that they did not know the 'real' Egypt; it is not just the Four Seasons Hotel, fancy clubs, wonderful dinners and beautiful houses. They did not know Egypt's villages or how the people living there felt when they could not afford to buy their children shoes for winter.

Egypt was living through Nazif's programme of economic reforms, but it was evident that the fruits of these changes would take time to trickle down to the working classes. It could easily have taken a decade or more and there was widespread despair in Egypt, coupled with a sense among the nation's citizens that they had no future. Things were tough and a lot of people felt they were not given a fair share of life. Until 2010, this was not widely recognised or reported. Mubarak was always concerned about mass demonstrations, so the trains, electricity, water and petrol were all subsidised. When I was minister, I commissioned a study that showed Egypt to be the cheapest country in the world for petrol. That was costing the country $10 billion a year in subsidies. I said these subsidies needed to change but Mubarak was not ready to action that change by beginning to gradually remove subsidies.

It was clear that something seismic was happening in the Middle East and I told my wife in early January 2011 that I thought Egypt would be next. I had said much the same a month earlier when I was in Italy with my nephew Ismail, an extremely bright and energetic young man known to all of us by his nickname, 'Simba', due to his love of Disney's *The Lion King* as a young child. The first protests of what became the Arab Spring had been held and he asked: 'Uncle, what do you think is going to happen to Egypt?' I replied that I thought that things were going to change. Mubarak was 82 and losing his grip, and I could sense his alertness had disappeared. So, when people in Egypt took to the streets on 25 January 2011, I was not at all surprised.

There were demonstrations, marches, occupations of plazas, non-violent civil resistance, acts of civil disobedience and strikes. Millions of protesters demanded the removal of Mubarak. Cairo was virtually a war zone and the port city of Suez saw frequent violent clashes. Protesters defied a government-imposed curfew. Watch groups were organised by civilian vigilantes to protect their neighbourhoods from looters. Violent clashes between security forces and protesters resulted in more than 800 deaths and 6,000 injured individuals. Protesters retaliated by burning over 90 police stations.

On 11 February 2011, Omar Suleiman, the vice president, announced that Mubarak had resigned. The Egyptian armed forces, headed by the effective head of state Mohamed Hussein Tantawi, announced two days later that the constitution would be suspended, both houses of parliament dissolved, and the military would govern until elections could be held. The previous cabinet, including Ahmed Shafik, would serve as a caretaker government until a new one could be formed.

Nazif was taken into custody in April 2011 on allegations of wasting public money, corruption and allowing others to profit but was acquitted by Egypt's highest court in 2016. Mubarak was tried on charges of negligence and failing to prevent the killing of protesters and sentenced to life imprisonment in 2012. However, this conviction was later overturned on appeal, which resulted in Mubarak and his sons being prosecuted instead, for corruption in 2015. He was held in a military hospital until he was acquitted of these further charges, along with his sons, in 2017. He died in February 2020, receiving a military burial at a family plot outside Cairo.

After a period of rule by the Supreme Council of the Armed Forces, the Muslim Brotherhood took power in Egypt through a series of popular elections, with Mohamed Morsi elected to the presidency in June 2012. However, the Morsi government encountered opposition after his attempt to pass an Islamic-leaning constitution. Mass protests broke out against his rule on 28 June 2013, and five days later he was deposed. General Abdel Fattah El Sisi went on to become Egypt's president after a 2014 election.

The Arab Spring obviously had a huge international impact. Europe had to deal with a refugee crisis on a scale hitherto unknown. There was a failure in the rule of law and the consequences were widespread, inspiring populist movements across Europe, and, in my view, playing a role in Brexit, Britain's departure from the European Union.

After the revolution, I did not go back to the country for a long time. Rawya and Yasseen also moved to Britain and Youssef relocated to France. There was just too much scapegoating going on. I was one of the only ministers appointed from the private sector who was not charged or convicted with crimes by the new regime. I had done nothing wrong, but my decision to leave the ministerial position in 2009 and relocate to the UK, two years before the revolution and subsequent prosecutions of serving ministers, may have helped secure my liberty.

My cousin Ahmed, one of the most honest and honourable men you could ever meet, was not so fortunate. He ended up in an Egyptian prison after the revolution. Also imprisoned were the steel magnate Ahmed Ezz, who was the party whip; Garrana, Abaza and El Fiqqi, who had all served with me in the cabinet; and Nazif. Two ministers – Rachid Mohamed Rachid and Youssef Boutros-Ghali – who were out of the country were tried in absentia. All are now free men.

But all that is in the past now. I return to Egypt when I can, and I think the country has improved a great deal in recent years. When I return to Egypt, I can see that there has been significant investment in the country's infrastructure, from new roads, bridges and public transport to newly developed cities. With an ever-growing population, and amid inflation imported from overseas, the challenges facing the country today are considerable: mitigating the rising cost of living, managing population growth, increasing job creation and investing in better healthcare and education. However, for all those issues, Egypt remains a great country and will always be my home.

I am proud to be able to say that, for an extraordinary period of my life, I served my country.

١.

CHAPTER TEN

Keeping it in the family

'A man's reach should exceed his grasp' is a refrain by the poet Robert Browning which has always inspired me. I like the image of someone stretching further than they thought their fingers and arms could reach to make that crucial difference. It is a bit like God's finger stretching out in the famous fresco on the ceiling of the Sistine Chapel. It is about reaching new goals, trying to go beyond your comfort level, and always trying to make your best better. It encapsulates my personal philosophy of always progressing for my family and my business.

Over the last 40 years, we have grown one of the largest family businesses in the Arab world that spans from China to Uganda and sells everything from burgers to bulldozers. But after leaving the ministerial office, I wanted a fresh challenge and I needed to do something new. I was restless in my desire to achieve something more.

I decided to take some of the fruits of our labour, the capital which we had made, and set up a private investment firm, Man Capital, in London. I chose a city I love and know well and, of course, it helped that I am fluent in English. My father had studied at Cambridge and developed a love of Britain then that, combined with us visiting London so frequently as children, resulted in a generational relationship that linked the two countries and allowed me to feel at home in the UK.

There is one and only London: unique, vibrant, safe and welcoming. There are cities that are magnetic and particularly attractive to people from our part of the world and London is one of them. It is up there with New York, Paris and Rome, but because of my family's links and our way of life, I was convinced, and still am, that London is the right place to base our investment business.

Logistics were an important factor and so too was the country's legendary rule of law. The English legal system is a solid anchor to anyone and to everyone. Also, I like how nobody in the UK gives a damn who you are. You have your privacy. I have been to countries where it is not advisable to talk freely in a hotel room. In such places, you cannot criticise anything, even if you are a foreign citizen or a diplomat. But in the UK, as long as you abide by the law, you are accepted. That's why it's a haven for people around the world. We are very glad to have made London our centre.

When I was running Mansour Automotive and Mantrac, I was preoccupied with how many cars and tractors we sold on a day-to-day basis. I did not pay enough attention to my personal investments and assets. My private bankers would simply tell me how much my assets had gone up or down in value each year. The family had cash from the profits of our various businesses, but that would go to the banks managing our portfolio. It was not a satisfactory arrangement as we never quite knew who was managing our money and did not feel in control.

I took a trip to America with Loutfy and Yasseen to meet with senior executives on Wall Street in Manhattan. I had befriended Lloyd Blankfein, who was CEO of Goldman Sachs, the investment bank, at that time. Lloyd arranged an introductory meeting for Loutfy and me with some of the bank's private equity and hedge fund clients. I was being showcased as a prospective investor. Loutfy and I sat around a table with around 20 investment managers, who introduced themselves and revealed the size of their respective funds. By the time they had finished there must have been $200 billion in assets represented. I joked, 'Well I should probably get up and leave!' These funds were perhaps beyond us at that stage, but after the meeting was over, one of the attendees came up to me and said, 'I know who you should meet.' The person he recommended was Bill Ford, the CEO of General Atlantic (GA), a private equity firm. I reached out to Bill and we arranged to meet for breakfast when he was next in London. We sat together in the restaurant of the Jumeirah hotel where he told me about the firm. I was immediately impressed and committed to invest with him right there and then.

As well as the GA referral, we returned from New York with

lots of ideas and advice. I felt that, with the right team, we could generate returns far greater than we were getting from private bankers and asset managers. We also would be in control in a way we were not before.

At that time, family offices were not widely used or well-known, so I began to visit some and ask for advice. It was a bit of an eye-opener. One family office seemed to have been set up entirely to service the needs of the wife and children of a wealthy man. I told my people that this was not the kind of family office I wanted. If my family desires theatre tickets, I can buy them myself. We decided that our model would be closer to the large single-family offices in New York, which are run like sophisticated private equity houses, but, crucially, without some of the down-sides. Private equity firms are constantly under pressure to raise and deploy capital. We had the benefit of time. We decided to pursue about one or two deals a year, generally looking to acquire stakes in private businesses across a range of sectors. We would deploy patient capital, investing truly for the long-term, backing companies, management teams and sectors that most closely matched our investment thesis. It would be incredibly exciting.

Loutfy worked with me on a strategy and we recruited a team of about a dozen investment management professionals, advisers and other staff. I said to them: 'What do banks offer that we cannot?' We did not want to spread ourselves too thinly. The technology industry would go on to be a big focus, but we were also keen to follow opportunities in education, healthcare, real estate and telecoms, among other areas.

Bill Ford also had a connection to another great business that we have invested capital in, Iconiq Capital. I was visiting California on business when I met with a guy in a leather jacket from South Africa who wanted to sell me a winery in Napa Valley. I dismissed the wine investment but later that day he called me while I was taking a walk, and said, 'There are a few people who I'd like you to meet in San Francisco.' I was driven to a pleasant, if unremarkable, building a few blocks from the financial district. A receptionist behind a glass screen directed me to the first floor, where I sat with the principals around a big conference table. They said they invested capital on behalf of high-net-worth individuals including some very well-known figures from across Silicon Valley and Hollywood. If true, it was an impressive client roster. They also mentioned that GA's Bill Ford was on their board, so that evening I called Bill and asked him if these guys were for real. He assured me they were, and we went on to invest with them.

Opportunities like these would never have crossed my path had I stayed in Egypt. For the most part we have invested directly in businesses on a private equity basis. Some family offices allocate very large shares of their portfolio with external managers, like private equity or hedge fund firms. But with only a few exceptions – including GA and Iconiq – we have managed our capital directly. Over time we have tended to divest from third-party funds, partly due to high fees and low returns. But, also, because we want to deploy our capital ourselves rather than through intermediaries. I always said that if they can do it, then there is no reason why we cannot.

The first investment we made on our own was in the global shipping company Vanguard Logistics Services, which we acquired via its California-based parent company, OTS Logistics Group, in January 2012. This was a landmark deal for me, not only as it was the first acquisition for Man Capital, but also because to this day, in dollar terms, it remains Man Capital's biggest take-over and largest asset by value.

The business, which was founded by the New Zealand entre-preneur Sir Owen Glenn a decade earlier, was by the time we acquired it one of the largest shipping companies of its kind in the world. Today it has over 120 offices and a presence in more than 100 countries. This was one of the main things that appealed to me – owning Vanguard would help me to fulfil a dream of owning a business with a truly global footprint.

One of our investment team had heard positive things about Vanguard, prompting Loutfy to travel to Los Angeles to meet Owen. He was a tough, straight-talking Kiwi. As they prepared to take their seats in the meeting, Owen boldly told my son, 'Loutfy, if I am going to sell my business and you don't have $400 million, we shouldn't be sitting here.' Loutfy replied, 'This number doesn't scare us.' Despite that awkward beginning, the meeting went well enough for our talks to progress. Owen travelled to London, where we had a meeting in our office and then met again over dinner. Just as Owen had made that warning to Loutfy, it was now my turn. We knew that a private equity firm had been keen to buy the company, but Owen withdrew from the deal quite late in that process. Over dinner, I wanted to look him in the eye and judge whether he was serious about selling to us. 'Are you really going to sell?' I asked. I hoped he could tell that I could not be pushed around and recall him repeating the same phrase: 'I am going to sell . . . I am going to sell.'

The deal took many months to complete. Owen joined me in the south of France, where we both owned properties, and we continued the conversation in the warmth of the Riviera while, back in London, my team pored over the numbers. After we had provisionally agreed a price, we realised the business had taken on more debt than we originally thought, but this was only a hiccup. After a few days I called Owen and gave him our offer. He said: 'Okay, Mohamed, done!'

We knew we were buying the company close to or at the peak of its economic cycle, but we believed in the long-term growth potential of the business. To create additional value, we changed the governance structure, brought in new people and systems, including a new CFO, established a HR function and, through digital transformation, created new reporting systems and analytics. It was not an overnight success but that fits with our patient capital approach – we build businesses and we knew we would get there.

Loutfy led this effort superbly and added to the leadership team by installing some very seasoned business leaders on the board, including the former Caterpillar group president Gerard Vittecoq; the former chair of GM Egypt, Rajeev Chaba; the former minister for finance in Egpyt, Youssef Boutros-Ghali; and career logistics leader Onno Meij, who was later appointed CEO.

Gerard has also been appointed to the board of Mansour Automotive and continues to make an extraordinary contribution. At
Vanguard, gradually profitability increased, peaking again in 2021,
partly as a result of the disruptions to the supply chain caused by
the Covid-19 pandemic that sent rates higher. Like the cargo ships
that carry our customers' goods around the world, the journey has
sometimes been hit by stormy weather and rough seas. But Vanguard is on course.

We have owned Vanguard now for more than a decade,
reflecting our long-term investment thesis. I would never rule out
selling a company or a stake in a business, but this is not what
drives me. I don't have a philosophical objection to selling something when the price is right, but I prefer to hold assets for the
long term and, to date, I have not disposed of any of our companies. Sometimes we may reduce our stake in a company, but the
more common route is for us to inject further equity. We want all
our portfolio companies to grow, and we will grow with them for
the long term.

The Vanguard investment has proved unusual in two respects:
it is the only logistics company we own, and one of the very few
businesses that we acquired outright. It was also rare in terms of
buying a business from a founder who did not remain heavily
involved in the day-to-day running of the business. Over the subsequent years our strategy has evolved. Today we are much more
likely to invest as minority shareholders and back founders who
will take the business forward.

I liked Owen, we established a rapport and he could be very

funny. But it seemed to me that he had run his business with an iron fist. So, when we are sizing up an investment, the character of the founder or leader is as important as the idea, concept and strategy, if not even more important. I look for companies with founders I respect and talented, entrepreneurial teams that we can help grow. We provide capital but feel we have a great deal more to offer through our experience of building and managing businesses. That becomes a very powerful tool and gives us a real opportunity to leverage our expertise, which is not just money but the human capital that we have as well: people, teams, systems and processes. Helping these businesses to develop takes vision and foresight.

Two other investments in which we took significant minority stakes in particular stand out – Inspired Education Group, founded by Nadim Nsouli, and Caffè Nero, managed by Gerry Ford. Along with Vanguard, these are among our largest investments and completing both transactions was largely down to the tireless work of Loutfy and the team.

We source most of our deals ourselves. We have found that you create your own deal flow; as a family office you cannot just rely on others such as investment bankers or private equity funds to bring you timely opportunities. We focus on a sector, build a network of founders and entrepreneurs, and do our own research and due diligence. There are no shortcuts or quick wins.

This was how we developed the opportunities with Inspired Education and Caffè Nero. We were able to establish a rapport with Nadim and Gerry, who are among a rare breed of business leaders who demonstrate good judgement, inspire the troops, are proactive problem-solvers, energetic and driven. We are long-term investors and we knew those individuals were people we could work with for many years.

Inspired Education is an international network of private schools that Nadim, a former banker and private equity investor, founded in 2013. The opportunity to invest in education was compelling. Armies defend nations but education builds nations. We knew that Nadim and his wife had suffered the most enormous tragedy when their eldest daughter, Lyla, died of brain cancer at the age of two, and that he had set up a charity to find a cure for that most devastating of all cancers in her memory. Loutfy got to know Nadim after meeting him at a London gym and the two struck up a friendship. When Loutfy discussed Inspired with me and later introduced me to Nadim, I knew almost immediately that this was someone I wanted to invest with. He would come to the same London gym as me and I joked that he was like an 'iron man', someone incredibly driven and on a mission to transform lives. I said to Loutfy, 'We should invest in a man like that. Do it.'

We were among Inspired's first investors. The plan at the time was to turn a small network of four schools into eight, and possibly to ten. But we shared Nadim's energy and ambition and felt the opportunity was far greater. There are now over 80 schools across five continents, and we have continued to invest capital and provide operational and strategic support. There have been many opportunities for us to exit the business with a very healthy return, but we are patient capital investors and it is a project that we want to be a part of for the long term. The support we have provided has included helping the business to enter Bahrain and Egypt, where there are plans for six new schools, the first of which will be established in the Palm Hills development in Cairo.

These establishments are, as the name implies, inspiring places of learning. When I visited one of their schools in the UK, its buildings and grounds reminded me of one of my favourite television shows, *Downton Abbey*! This is an organisation that now has many heavyweight backers and is clearly going places. When we invested in 2013, Inspired Education was valued at about €100 million; at a fundraising round in 2022 the enterprise was valued at €4.5 billion, which is an amazing return in under a decade.

With Gerry I knew I had encountered a man with vision and direction and who had a credible growth plan. I see Caffè Nero and its sister business, Coffee #1, which we are also invested in, as having enormous potential. There are maybe three or four main players in the coffee business – including Starbucks, which is publicly traded; Costa Coffee, which was sold to Coca-Cola for £3.9 billion in 2021; and Caffè Nero, which was founded in 1997 and is now the largest independent chain in the world, with a growing number of stores across Europe and on the east coast in the USA.

Like the independent educational sector, we think that coffee has huge growth potential. We knew that Gerry had never accepted outside capital, apart from friends and family, but we met him several times and we clicked. I liked him immediately, he is direct and open, as we are, and our relationship quickly blossomed. Where other investment firms had been rebuffed, Gerry welcomed us and saw us as potential long-term partners.

The Nero Group now operates over 1,000 stores across ten countries, including more than 650 Caffè Nero stores in the UK that employ over 6,000 people. We told Gerry we wanted to put our patient capital to work to help him deliver on his vision and mission.

We may have bought in when the coffee retail sector was at its pre-Covid-19 peak, around 2019, but we had no way of knowing that a pandemic would soon force the closure of coffee shops around the world. However, Gerry managed the business incredibly well during the pandemic. He is one of those people who acts, rather than reacts. On one occasion he visited me at my house after lockdown restrictions were lifted and I told him, 'Gerry, we are with you.' We assured him that he had our backing and our support. We would get through the pandemic and things would quickly bounce back.

The sector was hit hard but we were impressed by Nero's capabilities and how they responded and how hard they worked to get through it. As far as we were concerned that solidified our partnership even more. Loutfy travelled with Gerry to the US to see the rollout of stores there and returned even more optimistic about the future, while innovations including home delivery and pick-ups via tech platforms, and new products like canned coffee and branded coffee, showed that the company was not resting on its laurels. Coffee won't go away but you have to build an experience to encourage people to return to the stores.

I am excited about the coffee investments, although, ironically, I am an avid tea drinker myself. I drink at least 20 cups a day and as I have grown older, I have started drinking green tea. One of my favourite times of the day is when I prepare a cup for myself as the sun is rising. I struggle with caffeine, and I never drink it after about three o'clock as it affects my sleep. I sometimes struggle to sleep as it is, as my mind is always whirring.

I won't list all our investments, but another notable one that I should mention came to us via my dear friend Rajeev Chaba, who sits on several of our boards. Rajeev suggested I meet his nephew, Ruchir Arora, who had founded an interesting business in India in 2015 called CollegeDekho, which offers a portal for young men and women in India to find and apply to universities. We met at our office in London and we agreed to put in $2 million as an initial investment into the company. CollegeDekho has grown strongly off the back of further funding rounds, which we have participated in and maintained a sizeable share.

While the backbone of our portfolio comprises investments in brick-and-mortar businesses like Vanguard, Inspired and Caffè Nero, in terms of volume the biggest of our investment sectors is technology. We started small but over time have increased our focus on this sector significantly.

Our tech investment portfolio got off to a very strong start. Sherif Wahba, an investment banker at Goldman Sachs, called to say he had a suggestion. 'There is this Facebook company. Have you heard of it?' he asked. I had heard the name but not much else as I had been so busy running the ministry. Goldman had been given a mandate to try to create some liquidity for Facebook before it pursued a stock market flotation. I committed a considerable sum of money in dollars on this one telephone call, basically on instinct. The price I paid was $18 a share – less than one-fifteenth of the value that Facebook's shares would eventually reach as the company grew. Several years later, I sold this investment for a substantial profit.

The success of this investment gave us encouragement and soon J.P. Morgan was on the line with the offer of some pre-IPO stock in a company called Twitter. We invested there too and, as our appetite for these technology stocks and the significant liquidity that we invested in them became better known, more opportunities came our way. We went on to buy stakes in Spotify, Snowflake, Grab and Oakstreet Health, among others. In terms of multiples, my best investment was in Snowflake, a cloud-computing company whose stock rose to 30 times the price I paid. Of course, we did not know that such equities were the foothills of one of the biggest stock market booms of all time, but we made some smart investments and started to develop a reputation.

I first went to Silicon Valley, California, in 2014 and found it to be a completely different world. It was evident that significant changes were taking place in the way that human beings connect, transact, work and play. I was knocked out by the dynamism, energy and entrepreneurialism. I sat in my hotel watching the world go by with billionaires coming in for breakfast wearing jeans and trainers. It made a deep impression on me. But once I had got over the culture shock, my next question was, 'How could we become part of this?' Our business had been like a steady and reliable train. How could we stoke the fire of growth or find it a new engine?

We had done very well with our investments in Facebook and Twitter, but this was an area I really wanted to better understand. I asked Sherif to arrange some visits to venture capital firms in the area. I would go to their offices in my usual smart suit, tie and polished leather shoes, and would be greeted by young-looking men and women who seemed dressed for the beach. I recall taking off my tie in one meeting and talking for an hour about Egypt and Africa. The venture capitalists seemed fascinated and asked a lot of questions. 'I would like to invest with you,' I said at the end of the meeting, but then the mood changed. Their funds were fully subscribed, they told me. They would let me know when they needed to conduct any future fundraising. Other meetings followed a similar course.

I was left feeling confused and frustrated. As we were driven away from one meeting, I said to Sherif: 'Why did they take a meeting when they had nothing to sell?' Then I received a message from one of the firms we had met, asking if we could arrange a lunch. I thought there would be no harm in meeting them again. They told me that the reason they took the original meeting with me was because they had heard a lot about the Mansour Group and what it was doing in Africa. They were aware that they were under-invested in Africa and the Middle East and so they wanted my advice about whether to invest in certain assets there. That was another eye-opener to me. These venture capital guys were not really interested in my money. It was my insights that they wanted.

We got an appointment with Airbnb. I had heard a little

about how this company was exploring an interesting opportunity to allow people to monetise spare rooms in their properties. I was intrigued and, if the venture capital funds were not going to give us access to their investments, maybe we could take a more direct route. Sherif called Jeff Mullen, Airbnb's head of treasury, who asked if we could come over, so we drove to San Francisco and when we arrived at Airbnb's building, there was another culture shock. In the building's sizeable lobby were casually dressed young people and someone was even walking a dog. It reminded me of my college days in North Carolina.

At first, Jeff seemed most interested in asking about the Middle East and Africa, but then he started tapping on his BlackBerry – he was messaging Airbnb's chief financial officer, Laurence Tosi, and asking him to join us. Laurence soon arrived, we chatted a little and then I told him that I wanted to invest in the company. At first, I received the venture capital answer that the firm had plenty of funds from its last investment round and did not need to raise any more. Then Laurence looked at me and asked: 'How much do you want to put in?' I gave him a number and we took it from there. Airbnb became part of the portfolio.

The deals kept coming. We looked at a young taxi-hailing business called Uber and eventually invested with them too. I got to know Emil Michael, the Egyptian-born former special assistant to the US defence secretary Robert Gates in the Pentagon, who served during the Obama administration, and had become the right-hand man to Uber's co-founder and CEO Travis Kalanick. We developed a friendship, and I asked him for some advice because I was starting to think that I needed to have some kind of presence on the west coast of America. By then I was travelling to Silicon Valley about three or four times a year, leaving my suit behind these times and staying for around two weeks on each occasion. I found so much opportunity there that I began to think that we needed to organise ourselves in a different way. I decided that I needed somebody local who knew the area and the technology companies working there and could run the operation for me and help set up the investments. We had made some tech investments, but the logical next step would be to set up a venture capital business in California.

Emil put me in touch with Ramy Adeeb, an Egyptian-born, Harvard- and Stanford-educated software engineer and businessman who had formed an internet content company called Snip.it in 2011 while looking for a way to share relevant information regarding the Arab Spring uprisings. He had sold his company to Yahoo and although still young was already independently wealthy. He was familiar with the Mansour Group and was interested in meeting with me. However, having just sold Snip.it, he admitted he wanted to take a sabbatical from business. 'Ramy, think about it. I would like you to come and take this forward', I said.

I was incredibly impressed by Ramy's knowledge of the technology scene in Silicon Valley and elsewhere on America's west coast. He seemed to know everybody there. It was obvious that he was extremely bright, very well-connected and would be able to give us early access to opportunities in Silicon Valley that we lacked.

We went our separate ways, but he later gave me a call and said he was ready to help. 'The only reason I would do it,' he told me, 'is because of your name and good reputation in Egypt. I know that you are the sort of person I would like to work with.'

We agreed to create a venture capital firm together. Ramy came up with the name – 1984 Ventures, a reference to the iconic George Orwell-inspired advertising campaign for Apple's first personal computer. Loutfy went with some of my team to meet Ramy in Silicon Valley. They confirmed we should be the core and major investor in setting up 1984 Ventures. I encouraged him to recruit an advisory board, and he quickly found some very impressive people for us with years of experience in the technology sector. Apart from that, Ramy was left free to make other choices as he saw fit. It took us about six months to get the operation up and running, putting in seed capital. The strategy would be to invest seed or early stage capital in start-ups that were applying technology to large, established industries such as real estate, logistics and finance. On average, only about 15–20 per cent of venture capital deals make money. But 1984 Ventures has gone on to invest in more than 50 firms, of which around half have since come back for further rounds of investment from ourselves and other backers. For a venture capital firm, that is an amazing batting average. Overall, the fund is among the top performers in its category and we have already seen very good returns.

My time in California reaffirmed something that I had long realised – that the world needed to change, and digital businesses were going to be at the forefront. Our experiences at Man Capital were also a sign that our other businesses needed to change. We could not stagnate as a group. I had been at a Caterpillar dealer forum in 2005 when one of the speakers talked about how health-care was poised for a revolution and predicted online consultations alongside other sweeping changes. That assessment really struck a chord. He said digitalisation would change home entertainment, retail and how we interact as human beings. As our businesses span motor cars, supermarkets and fast-food restaurants, all this had deep implications for us. The only way forward was to lead from the front and my technology investments are an important and rewarding way of doing so.

We took risks, of course, with 1984 Ventures and Man Cap-ital. I always say that luck plays a role in life and I do consider myself to be a lucky man. There is an old Egyptian saying: 'Give me an inch of luck versus an acre of knowledge' and it is true. Of course, some of our investments have not gone as well as others. We invested in an e-cigarettes brand, which we had to exit at a loss. I lost a six-figure sum investing in bitcoin in 2018. I am a big believer in Warren Buffett's philosophy that if you are going to invest in something for the long term, you really do have to under-stand it. Perhaps I could have stayed in that bitcoin investment for longer, but you cannot win them all. Even Uber had some issues but we remained their investors for an extended period.

I have loved backing so many tech start-ups because I am always thinking about new trends and developments and how they will impact the world. I like to host breakfast meetings at my London home with people from business and the arts, among other sectors. Meeting smart and interesting people gives us a very rounded and informed view, which ultimately helps us when thinking about the future and the kinds of investments we may go on to make. Sourcing deals is not what these meetings and events are about, but every gathering is fascinating and useful. Yes, Man Capital has been a good investment, but it is also an opportunity to learn more about the world and where humanity is heading. It has been an amazing ride.

CHAPTER ELEVEN

Passion projects

What started it all? What defined it? Was it worth it? Such alarming questions sometimes pop up at three o'clock in the morning as I lie in bed thinking back on 50 years of working in our family business, and what did I learn and what can I pass on to the next generations. We rose. We sank. We fought back and were sunk again, but like the phoenix we rose again and our one aim has always been to grow. Another fearful early morning thought is that the first generation make it, the second fake it, the third take it for granted and, finally, it is lost. We have gone so far on an incredible journey as the fortune creators, and I hope we have been guided by value rather than price. I always wanted and still want to make something that has a moral worth as well as monetary value.

To that end I think of Leo Tolstoy, one of the greatest novelists and perhaps the greatest moralist of them all, who was so transformative (influencing symbols of non-violent struggle like Mahatma Gandhi and Martin Luther King Jnr) as a result of his benign philosophy. He gets to the heart of the matter in what one can and should do. I come back to three things he wrote. Firstly, 'everyone thinks he can change the world, but no one thinks of changing himself.' Food for thought! Secondly, 'everything comes in time to those who know how to wait.' And thirdly, I like how he espouses bravery, individuality and moral strength: 'Wrong does not cease to be wrong because the majority share in it.'

There is something inherently advantageous in the family-owned, privately-held model of company ownership in terms of delivering social and environmental benefits. Society needs businesses to embrace sustainability, but ownership structures make it easier for some to think long-term in this way more than for others. We have known for many years of the link between family ownership and economic success. Research shows that privately-held family businesses on average perform better on some key economic indicators than public companies because they are generally more stable, more patient and less short-term in their approach. It is no surprise, or coincidence, that family businesses were early adopters of sustainability practices and environmental, social and governance principles. It is not about quick wins; it is about the bigger picture. That's the vision I continue to hold for our family and our businesses.

At every step of my journey from 'Mo' the struggling waiter to someone with business interests across several continents, I come back to family as what defines and drives me. That is how I have survived, thrived and strived, always with family at the heart and head of everything I do and aim toward. It is defining about my essence and my ethos. So, when I think of the first line of *Anna Karenina*, Tolstoy takes me to my core. 'All happy families are alike; each unhappy family is unhappy in its own way.' I have been lucky to have a family whose members agree on that. Our personal and business roots remain firmly in the mould that we are united and feed off each other's strengths and weaknesses into a way of complementing others, which also then becomes a strength.

I am not always strong on the detail, but I am good on central direction and broad brush strokes. Youssef is masterful with detail and uses that strength for brilliant strategic and tactical execution of ideas and ambitions. We are united in the family, making decisions together and when we disagree, we sort that out behind closed doors and always come to a decision going forward. We obviously only want the first half of the Tolstoy edict – to be a happy family – and so far that desire has translated into a contented force the moves forward as one unit.

Back to my three o'clock moment: *What have we achieved, how did we get there, and was it all worth it?* After all the millions of hours, struggles, and ups and downs that have taken a toll there is also an immense feeling of reward and responsibility; I think a bit of soul-searching always brings new bearings and understanding.

In some ways, our lucky break started with an almost child-like love of cars. I was probably no more than three years old when I would play with model cars, learning all the makes and models of Buicks and Chevrolets. I did so with an intense passion that only a child truly can obsess over and which in turn lasts a lifetime. I did not know that my fortune would be spurred and triggered by this obsession with the beauty and power of cars or that I would build a business around Chevrolets, whose early maxim when the company started in America was 'a car for every purse and purpose.' Chevrolet became the volume leader in the General Motors family, selling mainstream vehicles to compete with Henry Ford's Model T in 1919, its Chevrolet International becoming the bestselling car in the US by the end of the 1920s. It epitomised the American Dream and I wanted a part of it.

Inspiration and aspiration are two corner stones of my life. I was hooked on the romance, revs, rip-roaring noise and beauty of cars. Also, how it was a symbol of prosperity and the magic of technology, which made me leap in without any hesitation when the chance to be part of the automobile industry came our way. That the Chevrolet would be tied to my family name was not even a fleeting hope when my love affair with cars started because I was so young.

It is no small irony that a car was also the cause of an almost fatal accident when I was run over aged ten and had to spend three years in bed. But the flip side of life is death and the split-second difference between the two is a shadow and a constant reminder of where we are and what can occur. And I suppose my point about my auto obsession is that nothing comes out of nowhere, and cars were parked in my imagination from the start.

Dreams can be the trigger and foundation for transformation

and cars were exactly that for me. Those early days of holding small models in my hand, racing them on the carpet, my imagination stirred when with a grown-up at the wheel and his pedal to the metal all were a pathway to dream and hope. I ended up employing thousands of people in the auto industry, selling hundreds of thousands of cars, and trading across African countries. The dream and the reality started by the motor engine go on. Electric transport is my current obsession, and it too is fuelled by dreams and ambitions. I am hoping this too will speed and further my family's constant desire to keep moving and to be on a pathway for growth.

My second passion as a child was football. My home-spun theory is that what you do or like as a child has a far greater effect on what you do or can do as an adult. I was never going to play football for Egypt or Manchester United but in every football fan's secrets and dreams they are at some time winning or saving the goal that defined their generation; that World Cup 1966 moment for England, or Egypt's triumphs in the first two African Cups of Nations at the end of the 1950s. Seeing kids knock balls about in the dusty streets of Alexandria or on the white beach by the Mediterranean was a spur for fun and endless conversations; nothing quite unites the planet like sport, particularly football. In a back street in a bazaar in the smallest village in Egypt the words 'Manchester United' or 'Liverpool' are as likely to echo as those of Egypt's great clubs, Al Ahly or Zamalek. Those clubs' names conjure up heroism, wizardry, transformational opportunities and riches beyond dreams. The magic of how two studded feet and a piece of spherical leather could transform into a formula of motion, money and magic, capturing the minds, imagination, hopes and dreams of so many millions. And is, also, a trillion-dollar industry. For me, 'the' team was and is Manchester United while my son Loutfy supports Chelsea. We joke, bond, compete, argue, agree and disagree, but always endlessly follow the game while sticking passionately to the support of our chosen teams.

Football is a love and an obsession for literally all of us: in the family, it is cars and football that are what we like and discuss. As it turned out, both played key roles in what we did in business and what has inspired us. Those moments when we question ourselves in a dark way can, for me, be met with light and inspiration in the eruption of a football crowd or the roar of a Ferrari engine. So, with one foot on the pedal and another thumping a leather ball, these two passions combined into my love for business which led to my being lucky enough to do well enough to share our success through philanthropy.

I still enjoy going to work every morning but, if you can co-ordinate investments around your passions, that is the Holy Grail. I have been fortunate enough in both my career and investment journey to be able to achieve this, and the excitement I get from aligning passion and profit is one of my greatest privileges. As I have always been fanatical about the 'beautiful game' the chance to use football to sponsor and market my deals for Mansour Automotive and Chevrolet was a dream combination.

In some ways, I also have football in my blood – thanks to my Uncle Mostafa, the legend that he was in Egyptian football. He was my mentor and I loved him dearly. The obituaries when he died in

2002 called him a 'trailblazing keeper' and 'one of the leading figures in Egyptian football.' He was proud of how African football had progressed during his lifetime and believed that the World Cup would one day be won by an African nation. My brothers and sister, sons, nephews and nieces share this passion for football.

During one of Loutfy's trips to sub-Saharan Africa in 2013, he came across the Right to Dream (RTD) football academy in Ghana, a global organisation enabling greater access to education, opportunity and equality through football. It was built on the vision of a football coach and social entrepreneur called Tom Vernon, who set it up with 16 youngsters in Ghana in 1999. Tom realised that it was not only a lack of qualified football coaches or decent facilities that was preventing the young players he encountered from progressing – he could see that many also needed better housing, schooling, diet and healthcare. He saw how football can lift the best footballers out of poverty and harsh social conditions. But he did not just want to teach youngsters how to play football; his vision was to use a football academy as a platform to inculcate values, integrity and good citizenship in the community. Any young person who failed to make it as a professional footballer would have a first-rate education to fall back on. And all students would be encouraged to create opportunities for others. Loutfy and I were more than impressed. We wanted to be part of it.

The results of Tom's visionary approach and the structures that he built speak for themselves. Just taking that original group of 16 boys, three went on to play for their country, five played professionally, while another six graduated from leading US universities thanks to fully funded athletic scholarships. Since then, more than 150 RTD students have become professional footballers, 40 of whom have played for their countries. RTD opened a second academy in Denmark in 2016 after it completed a ground-breaking deal to acquire a European premier league club, buying FC Nordsjalland (FCN), based in eastern Denmark, for €10 million.

Our engagement started in 2013 by helping to build eight football pitches, loaning them eight Caterpillar excavators for six months. Fast forward to today and we own the organisation. On one level it is an investment in our portfolio, but more than that we feel, and know, that sport gives purpose to people. It gives happiness to the people playing and supporting it by bringing people together. It is something that is unique. It gets people on the right track of life.

Several players from the academy in Ghana have been signed by Ajax in Amsterdam, including Mohammed Kudus. His Ghanian teammate Kamaldeen Sulemana joined the French club Rennes in 2021 and then moved to English Premier League club Southampton in 2023. Brentford player Mikkel Damsgaard, the talented winger who scored from a free kick for Denmark in a European Championship semi-final against England in 2021, was a graduate of RTD's Danish academy and a former player for FCN, which has one of the youngest teams in Europe, with an average age of 20. RTD have won the title of the prestigious Gothia Cup youth tournament held annually since 1975 in Gothenburg, Sweden, six times, with the success of its under-17 team in 2022 bringing RTD their fourth consecutive title win. At the 2022 men's World Cup in Qatar, seven RTD graduates made appearances, including Kudus, Sulemana and Damsgaard.

But the impact goes beyond the football field. The RTD Academy in Ghana is a school, committed to teaching general classes, as well as a football academy. Over 120 students have received student-athlete scholarships at high schools and universities in the US and the UK with a value exceeding $25 million. In the case of FCN, the club is run as a non-dividend, while 1 per cent of player and staff salaries and stadium revenues are donated to Common Goal, the football industry charity. I was so impressed by the work of Common Goal that I donated $2 million in 2022. What is hugely important to us is that the academies are educating the students and preparing them for their adult lives, as well as helping them to develop their football skills. I was fortunate to meet some of Right to Dream's brightest and best at a dinner in New York in 2022, including Firas Kora from Benin, who is our first student to attend an Ivy League School in America – he is currently studying politics, philosophy and economics at the University of Pennsylvania. I also met Adelaide Armah, who is currently studying sociology at Bates College in Maine, and Ousseni Bouda from Burkina Faso, who plays for San Jose Earthquakes in the MLS and is studying international relations at Stanford University in California. I was so impressed with them all, and meeting them reaffirmed why we wanted to invest in the organisation and our long-term commitment to it.

It was so important to me that one of the next big investments in RTD happened in Egypt. For many the dream is to emulate Mo Salah and become a superstar of the world game. Salah is a hero in Egypt and practically brings the country to a standstill when he plays for Liverpool FC in the English Premier League. He is an inspiration to many who want to meet their dreams. There may have been other Egyptian footballers who were as naturally talented, but he worked hard to make his dream a reality. My vision is to build in Egypt a trigger for sport and life change. Egypt has been the most successful national football team on the African continent. However, Salah aside, not many Egyptian footballers have gone on to become global stars.

That is why, as this book was being written, construction work continued on a new RTD academy west of Cairo at Palm Hills' new Badya development. I visited the new academy in April 2023 as work continued at the facility. Scheduled to welcome students in the summer and officially open towards the end of 2023, the RTD Egypt Academy is meticulously designed with top-notch football facilities and residential and educational buildings, all crafted to maximise the development of student-athletes and offer aspiring young talents in Egypt a world-class experience. RTD Egypt makes me so proud and it was a delight to meet some of the 60 students in the academy's first intake, who made it through a series of try-outs that attracted some 60,000 young people.

Importantly, RTD is investing in its women's and girls' programmes alongside the programmes for male athletes. The Egypt academy has a women's football team, called TUT FC, which began playing in the Egyptian Premier League in 2022. They won the Egyptian Women's Cup in 2023, overcoming adversity by defeating finalists Amereya YC with four players suffering from flu and another playing despite having a broken nose. For goalkeepers in Egypt, we are going to have a scholarship scheme under Uncle Mostafa's name. So, the DNA and thinking behind RTD is a shared dream. Investing in the young people of Egypt is incredibly important for me and my family and we look forward with excitement and optimism to see what RTD Egypt will produce for years to come.

• • •

However, the next phase of the RTD expansion is, if anything, even more exciting. It is a new American 'Dream' for me, my family and for Right to Dream.

Ever since buying Right to Dream in 2021, I wanted to expand the organisation to the US. It seemed such a natural fit, not least when considering how many former RTD students have gone on to play soccer professionally in America or study at the country's great colleges or universities. The ties were there and the alignment in values and in the approach that the US takes to college sport made it the perfect fit for us. We looked initially at Baltimore, Maryland, but could not quite make that venture work. Then we learned about a unique opportunity in San Diego, and when we took a closer look, we realised immediately that it ticked all the boxes from a purpose as well as a commercial perspective.

And so it was that in May 2023, in front of an enthusiastic audience of flag-waving fans, city leaders, football executives and other well-wishers, we announced the launch of a new Major League Soccer (MLS) club in San Diego, California. As the ticker tape blew across the stage at a launch event at San Diego State University's newly-built Snapdragon Stadium, I had to pinch myself that one of the largest and most rewarding deals of my career had been completed.

The bare facts are as follows: we agreed to pay $500 million for the right to jointly own an MLS team in the city. The team will debut as the league's 30th team in February 2025 and play at the 35,000-seat Snapdragon Stadium, the largest non-NFL stadium in the MLS. We will invest at least a further $200 million to build an RTD academy and school and recruit players, coaches, commercial staff and other employees. We put the project together through a joint venture with the Sycuan Band of the Kumeyaay Nation, the first Native American tribe to part-own an MLS team. Also invested in the team is the baseball star Manny Machado of the San Diego Padres.

The Sycuan tribe had wanted to put an MLS team together for some time. We first started talking with them in 2022, and we immediately bonded. We knew we could work together. They share our values and commitment to investing in the future by supporting our youth. The San Diego-based club also cements the bond between Right to Dream and the MLS, building upon the foundation laid by the many talented RTD graduates who have already brought their skills and passion to the league.

There is much to do before the team starts playing. We have to give the club a name, for one – we will consult with local fans and others in the community – and also decide on the team's colours. But we are not setting off from a standing start. We expect some of the San Diego players to be recruited from across the RTD network, augmented by players scouted from across North America and Europe. Leading the organisation will be Tom Penn, the highly respected sports executive who previously was President and co-owner of LAFC, an MLS club in Los Angeles that was founded in 2014.

The deal attracted global media interest and coverage. Many of the articles in the British and Egyptian press reflected on the fact that it is the first MLS team to be part-owned by an Egyptian or British citizen, counterbalancing the trend of the last 10 years which has seen so many soccer assets in England and around the globe acquired by American firms and businesspeople.

In paying $500 million for the right to enter the MLS as the league's 30th team, we set a new bar for a new start-up team. Indeed, taking the franchise fee as a proxy for the club's valuation, this was arguably the sixth largest football club deal on record at the time – behind only Chelsea, AC Milan, Lyon, Manchester United and Arsenal in the pantheon of large-scale transactions. But we are very comfortable with that valuation – indeed in February 2023, even before our agreement with the MLS, *Forbes* estimated that the average value of the current 29 clubs in the MLS was $579 million, or $79 million more than we would go on to pay for the San Diego club.

San Diego has a number of unique selling points. As well as being a beautiful city with great climate that will appeal to players across the US and internationally, its location close to the border with Mexico gives us some real advantages. Students from across the border will be eligible to go to the academy thanks to a FIFA rule that permits football academies located within 31 miles of a neighbouring country to recruit within that country as well.

We also see huge potential for recruitment of players and staff, and hopefully some fans too, from south of the border, while the Latino community in southern California, renowned for its passion for soccer, is also a natural fanbase for the new team. We are mere custodians of a club that ultimately belongs to the city and the fans. San Diego, which is a market that has been under-served by major league sports ever since the Chargers moved their gridiron franchise to LA in 2017, will have an MLS club for generations to come.

There were large and diverse crowds at our launch events, which included a reception for local dignitaries at Sycuan's historic US Grant hotel, an official launch in front of the world's media, and culminated in a party for thousands at the stadium one joyous evening in late May 2023. It was so gratifying to see all the enthusiasm and positivity in the city, as reflected not only in the tone of the proceedings but also in the sheer numbers of people who came out to the events despite being given no more than about 24 hours' notice in many cases. It emphasised just how much passion there is for soccer in the city. San Diego already has a fine women's team, the San Diego Wave, which began play in 2022, and a competitive second-tier men's team, the San Diego Loyal, which made its debut in the USL Championship in 2020. We wish the Wave and the Loyal well, and hope that the addition of an MLS team will further grow interest in the sport in the city, benefiting everybody.

It has been several decades since San Diego's soccer fans have been able to watch a top-flight men's team representing the city, and you could see what it meant as we launched the venture. I lost count of the number of San Diegans who came up to me to shake my hand and wish us well. There is a long way to go but we could not have had a more positive start.

Onlookers at the launch events commented that they felt the warmth and respect among the partners in the venture, which was lovely to hear. I cannot over-state how much admiration and respect I have for the Sycuan tribe. It is an honour to be involved in this venture with them. I will always cherish the memory of the traditional dances and songs they performed in the Kumeyaay language at a ceremony at the reservation to bless our partnership. It moved some of us to tears and was such a privilege to see and hear it performed. Loutfy and I accepted beautiful and thoughtful gifts from the tribe: a bundle of white sage, which is sacred and used for burnt offerings and purification; abalone shell, a protected species due to its over-fishing that was once a staple in the Kumeyaay diet; a gourd used for water or oils; and a traditional Kumeyaay basket woven so tight it can retain water.

During the launch, Major League Soccer's visionary Commissioner, Don Garber, spoke movingly of the vision that we and Sycuan were able to bring to the venture. Describing it as a "truly historic moment for soccer in North America", Don said our ownership group represents everything that the MLS is all about – international expertise and success, a genuine local connection, and a belief in the ability of soccer to inspire and excite people. When he went on to say that our diverse ownership group embodies a "League for a New America", I could not have been prouder.

Don has witnessed the launch of many 'expansion teams' since he was first appointed to the role back in 1999 (the same year, coincidentally, that Tom Vernon established RTD), when the league had only 10 teams. The league has expanded three-fold and continues to set new records for attendance and broadcast revenue, and new standards for the fan experience which are the envy of the rest of the world. The MLS is fortunate to have Don as its leader and I look forward to working with him in the coming years.

As co-owner, I was honoured to take my seat on the Board of Governors of the MLS at a meeting in Washington DC in July 2023, alongside such other owners as Stan Kroenke (Colorado Rapids), Hank Paulson (Portland Timbers), David Tepper (Charlotte FC) and Steve Cohen (LA Galaxy), among others. In the MLS, the teams compete vigorously on the field of play, but off the pitch, there is a level of cooperation and collaboration between owners that is probably unique in world soccer and is very appealing. I am looking forward to working with the other Governors in ensuring that the league continues to go from strength to strength.

The field of play itself has become star-studded, featuring some of the greats of the game in recent years such as English Premier League stars Frank Lampard (NYFC), Steven Gerrard (LA Galaxy), Didier Drogba (Montreal Impact), Zlatan Ibrahimovic (LA Galaxy), Wayne Rooney (DC United) and Thierry Henry (New York Red Bulls). The signing to Inter Miami in 2023 of arguably the greatest footballer in the history of the sport – the Argentinian maestro Lionel Messi – represented another stunning endorsement for soccer in America and an unprecedented opportunity for the MLS.

The MLS always has attracted celebrity interest too – minority shareholders across the league include Reese Witherspoon (Nashville SC), Will Ferrell (LAFC), Matthew McConaughey (Austin FC) and David Beckham (Inter Miami). I can see why there has been so much investor interest in the league. The sport is certain to be given a huge boost before, during and after the 2026 men's World Cup, just as the 1994 World Cup in the USA left a lasting legacy - including the creation the following year of the MLS itself. The league is now considered one of the fastest growing in the world. Average attendances are around 25,000 and rising. Even before the Messi deal, the 10-year, $2.5 billion media partnership that the MLS agreed with Apple TV in 2022 was clear evidence of where the game is heading. In England we have seen the impact that a great broadcast partner can deliver to football and I have no doubt that Apple TV will do for the MLS what Sky Sports has done for the English Premier League. Then there is the fact that the MLS – in common with other major sports leagues in America – has a stable league, without promotion or relegation, which encourages long-term thinking and provides financial security and sustainability.

So we are hugely optimistic for the future of the sport in America – the sky truly is the limit – and we think the club's valuation will soar. But we will measure success in other ways, from the development of elite young players through our academy to the impact that the educational component will deliver. At the new club's inaugural board meeting in June 2023, I was struck by the sense of purpose, drive and forward momentum in the project. If we achieve only half as much in San Diego as Right to Dream has achieved in Africa and Europe already, I will be very satisfied.

At this stage of my life, that is the kind of legacy I want to leave to the city and the sport. It is just another significant staging point on a journey that started with helping RTD improve its playing facilities in Ghana in 2013, continued with our acquisition of Right to Dream in 2021 that financed upgrades to existing operations and a new academy and women's team in Egypt, and now has culminated in one of the biggest soccer club deals in history. It is a project that I hope will transform lives and unlock a world of new opportunities for young people in southern California and Mexico to chase their dreams.

• • •

Cars and football, not to mention bulldozers . . . are accelerators and motivators for social change. These are great passions of ours, as are new technologies, but not to an obsessional degree. I would hate it if a member of my family was the owner of a flashy Lamborghini and parked outside Harrods, or if we were involved with a football club that was perceived as putting money first and morals second. We are not perfect, but we know from our 50 years building businesses with people that good behaviour produces lasting results.

Abraham Lincoln once said: 'Nearly all men can stand adversity, but if you want to test a man's character, give him power.' Before modern buzzwords like 'stakeholder capitalism', 'sustainable development' and 'purpose' were widely adopted by business leaders, I was raised to think about how your actions should uphold high ethical and moral standards. In a commercial context, this means providing significant benefits to the communities and customers you serve by giving opportunities to people in developing countries and under-served communities. I grew up in an environment where I saw this operating in my father's business. He cared deeply for the people around him and acted to protect them and take care of them, through both good and bad times. He always tried to create a supportive environment.

Loyalty and kindness are not just words. Tolstoy knew that. I once heard on the radio someone saying, 'It's nice to be important but it's more important to be nice.' It is now one of my mantras.

Giving back through philanthropy brings immense reward and the seeds of that were sown by my father who has always been a great example of mine. He worked hard and gained much through that and, importantly, he twice lost the lot. But, whether going through good or bad times, he always gave to those less fortunate than him and said we must help others.

As a result of my father's teaching, I founded the Lead Foundation dedicated to provide loans to impoverished women in Egypt in 2003. The not-for-profit provides loans to women who are unable to access credit from commercial banks and other traditional sources. I was very grateful to Elizabeth Cheney, daughter of the then vice president Dick Cheney, for all the support she gave us. She had been a consultant to the United States Agency for International Development before she was appointed to a Middle East diplomatic role in the State Department in 2002 and was a strong supporter of the Lead Foundation and our application for funding from USAID.

Since its inception, our focus has always been in providing support to female entrepreneurs and small business owners and nearly 90 per cent of all our loans over the years – which amounted to around four million by the middle of 2022 to over a million borrowers – have been provided to women.

Most of our loans are group loans – small communities of women who pool capital and guarantee each other's credit. Generally, these are people not registered as self-employed with the authorities and thus would be unable to access traditional sources of finance. Our clients use the capital to buy a sewing machine, some other useful piece of equipment or something that they can use to make an honest and decent living. We also provide individual loans and insurance.

The organisation has branches throughout Egypt and functions rather like a bank. Many of the loan officers are women and make lending decisions based on the personal integrity of the applicant. It is relatively rare for our borrowers to get into arrears or fail to pay back their loans, but it does happen sometimes. In normal market conditions, the proportion of the loans that underperform is less than 0.5%, which is virtually nothing in the commercial banking sector, although there were increases in defaults after the 2011 revolution and during the Covid-19 pandemic. But, in general, very poor people pay back their debt better than some large corporates.

Nothing that I have done in my career has made me prouder than the work of the Lead Foundation. Its work is crucial.

• • •

You must have a passion for the business of being a family to stay as a family business because there are many pressures mounted against you. The advantages are your independence and flexibility but as families grow in number and get more difficult to manage, the interests do not always stay the same. Some members retain their passion for the business and others become more interested in the pay-outs it provides. This can be when problems arise, so a family must be very tight and focused for its businesses to survive.

The Mansour family is constantly expanding and there are now more than fifty of us. We keep the family united through blood bonds and business ties. Our aim is to be as tight as my siblings and I were to our parents. To that end, we have all signed a kind of unity charter as a symbol and legal agreement of our future bond and growth.

We have always been a close clan. We want the next generation's connection and communication to be unbreakable, just as it was and is between us siblings. Our family charter, or the 'Magna Carta', as we jokily call it, sets out guidelines for how sons and daughters should be funded as they grow into adulthood. They are all given a choice of whether they want to join the family business, and there is absolutely no obligation to do so. If they wish to work for and potentially help run one of our companies, they know they must start at the bottom. My unaltered belief is you cannot start too low. Remember that waiter Mo! On just $1.25 an hour.

One of my nephews flipped hamburgers in a McDonald's, another drove a truck for one of our supermarkets and a third sold car parts in a service station. Two of my nieces worked behind the till, learning who we value above everything: our customers. They were under no pretensions that they had to work hard, not simply at their jobs but also to be accepted by their colleagues. Just because they have Mansour as their family name it does not grant them one of the top positions.

All our businesses already have considerable ranks of well-qualified personnel, ready and trained to play their parts in our commercial world when they get a chance. Everyone across our businesses knows that they can have a decent career there, as well as in the larger group, but nothing will come automatically as they will have to earn every promotion. The whole process from bottom to top could take many years.

My wife and I told our children that it would be fine if they had wanted to be a doctor, painter or anything else, rather than enter the family business. Both my sons went to the same school, the Cairo American College in Egypt, from kindergarten to the age of 18. They both studied for bachelor's degrees in business administration in America, and both began their careers in banking during the boom that preceded the global financial crisis of 2008.

Both later joined Mantrac, before their paths diverged. Loutfy went on to be chief executive of Mantrac and Man Capital. Mansour had worked in a sales role for Mantrac in Cairo for about a year when he told me he wished to relinquish his role and step back from the business. He felt it was not his calling. I told him I would never expect him to do something that he did not enjoy or have a passion for. I accepted and respected his decision. He wants a quieter and more private life, and I can understand that. We are a well-known family, particularly in Egypt, and that is not always compatible with a desire for privacy. Mansour may no longer be involved in the day-to-day activities, but he remains very engaged and provides strategic input and advice that is invaluable. My father had expected, demanded even, that his children follow him into the family business. But it was a different time then and the world has changed so much, so too have we as a family. I want my children to be happy, choose their futures, map out the paths they wish to navigate and follow what is important to them.

We all contribute to the future and have a duty to our children and our grandchildren, the generations of people yet to come. My family is the most important thing to me and I will always offer them guidance and advice, as well as my support and love, which is permanent and unconditional.

I have read about other family businesses where there has been a lot of in-fighting and I have seen it destroy relationships and companies. It is all too common that this happens but it is usually because two different agendas emerge: one belonging to the people managing the business and the other reflecting the interests of shareholders who want profits and dividends. What happens in the latter circumstance if the business is growing and it needs its profits reinvested into its future in the short term? I know big family businesses where the shareholder register has swelled to hundreds of names. Only three or four of those people listed are involved in actually running the business, yet those others who are listed request more cash payments each year at the family's general assembly and do not understand why there needs to be investment. This approach inevitably leads to friction, division and inefficiency.

When I was young, our father gave my siblings and me four little pieces of wood, representing the four of us. 'You can break one by itself,' he would tell us, and watch us do so. We could break two and even three when the pieces were stacked together. But we could not break all four when held together. He wanted us to realise that we were unbreakable if we stayed together and were united. My brothers and I went to university together, lived together and even partied together. Through these experiences, we developed the strength that has made the Mansours who we are today. Envy and jealousy are not tolerated. We do not allow people to put wedges between us. Our parents taught us to be united, have principles, act in the correct way, be honest and hard-working. That is how we saw them behave and we continue to learn from each other.

The younger generation, however, are clearly much more technologically literate and more conscious of environmental issues, which we need to encourage. One of my nephews, Mohamed Ismail Mansour, started Infinity Renewable Energy, which operates one of the largest solar energy businesses in Africa. I am very proud of him. When he was getting started, he never came and said: 'Uncle, I need money.' He found his own funding, working first at McDonald's and then deciding to get the financing he needed and achieve what he wanted to achieve for himself. 'I want to do something on my own,' he told us. Almost a decade later, with the business well established, we were only too happy to invest through Man Capital.

The moment you forget the values you grew up with; the instant that you think that you can do no wrong; that is when you fail. A lot of businesspeople lose touch with themselves, their environment and their roots after they have tasted success. I have seen this a lot over the years. I am very comfortable with my life, but I am also always looking for the next idea. Passing on the baton is perhaps the most difficult part, so we are determined to get it right.

My brothers and I may have built the businesses, but we want our children and grandchildren to feel ownership over them too. It is natural for my siblings and me to begin to review some of the ownership structures in preparation for the next generation, and over the last few years this process has gradually evolved. For example, while we all remain shareholders in the automotive and Caterpillar businesses, I am no longer invested in the supermarket businesses, which are now run by Youssef's daughter Soraya Mansour, while Youssef has exited from Man Capital, McDonald's and Palm Hills. I have total confidence that Loutfy will continue to steer Mantrac and Man Capital forward successfully, and that Mansour Automotive will carry on going from strength to strength. Now underway, this reorganisation is inevitable and, we hope, will provide clarity and help to smooth the transition to the next generation. Through it all, however, those bonds that were forged through adversity and affection continue to bind my siblings and me together.

I hope that there will be continuity but, also, I trust that the next generations, if they do decide to go in a new direction, will find a formula that aligns with their interests and passions while preserving the essence of what we built and our parents wished to construct, while creating growth, unity and an unbreakable, collective sense of purpose.

Naturally, keeping what we have built as a family business has become a passion for me. Transforming our operations to being one step ahead in technology and investing in some of the brightest tech stars on the planet is something I could never have done if I had stayed solely operating the automotive and Caterpillar dealerships. When you have a family office, you have a passion for what other businesses you can get into. What is the world moving towards and how can you invest in new things? That is how we have got to where we are today. Would we have thought of investing in Right to Dream if we did not have the family office? Definitely not. Would we have thought of investing in education, logistics and coffee shops? No.

Of course football, excavators, cars and an architectural gem aside, work itself – in all the businesses that we operate – is an active and all-consuming passion of mine. Trying to constantly excel and be ahead of competitors drives me forward, but it does come at a price, which is the stress that one lives under. However, you have to weigh that against the happiness you – and hopefully others – feel when you succeed.

12

CHAPTER TWELVE

Legacy builders

They say home is where the heart is. Well, I would say that is true up to a point! Houses have happily as well as unhappily defined who we are as a family. We have lost homes, had houses taken from us through sequestration and one was even burned down in a time of revolution. Throughout our complex family history, we have had to abandon buildings, as well as countries. We have been emotionally drained but also elated by where we have lived.

So, I would say that home ownership is a double-edged sword: it provides sanctuary, safety and status, but its loss brings pain, penury and humiliation. I have never forgotten the shame of having to leave my rented frat house while studying at North Carolina State University after our family's cotton business was confiscated and all our income dried up. It was shocking to be forced to leave my home due to having no money. My father and mother experienced even worse hardship, even more starkly under Nasser's rule in Egypt, when everything they owned was taken away by the state.

Houses have often defined the Mansours' hopes and setbacks, in many ways mapping out our entire history. For that reason, there is no building more important to me than Dar al Mansour, our Cairo-based family home, a magnificent Italianate/Romanesque mansion where the most defining characteristic is its location with a truly remarkable view overlooking the Pyramids. It was all part of my ambition to build a residence of far greater significance than merely one man's family home. I wanted to build a residence that reflected and revived generations of family tradition and heritage. It is intended to be a hymn in architecture and the decorative arts to express my love and gratitude to my family and, also, my country.

It took 20 years for us to buy the land with my mother buying the first small plot, and I then slowly purchased more until we had a four-acre site. The criteria were that it had to be near to and have a view of the Pyramids. As a child I had ridden horses around those totemic triangles of stone built 4,000 years ago by an army of 125,000 workers. I, too, had travelled into the desert among the undulating dunes by the greatest river on earth that had defined and intrigued Egyptians for millennia. The unique point of the house, beyond its splendid architecture and its stunning interiors, was always to be its breathtaking view over those pyramids. These burial edifices with their triangular silhouettes on the horizon give a magical, mystical glimpse of the greatest architectural forms in history. We took ten long years to plan and execute the construction and complex engineering for Dar al Mansour. The early Egyptians were clearly a lot smarter, taking just 30 years to finish one of the Seven Wonders of the World without a Caterpillar or electricity!

I wanted the house to be a tribute to my family's roller-coaster past, a respectful nod to the houses that my grandfather and great-grandfather had gained and lost in the turmoil of harsh economic and political crosswinds. It was also in gratitude to my father who had taught me everything I knew about graft and growth in business which, of course, pay for houses. The Bible's famous 'In my father's house are many mansions' quotation refers to spiritual reward but, for me, it is simply a reflection on the relationship between fathers and sons and their forbears as the past, present and future interconnect. The future is determined by what we do in the present today which in turn is influenced by the past.

Inspired by my mother's natural flair for design, this dream house in Egypt was completed in 2016. Realising the full promise of this passion was helped in no small part by my sister Rawya, whose design expertise and eye for detail were major drivers in bringing it to completion. Learning its ancient stories helped nurture in me a deep love of Egypt's history.

After my mother had found and acquired the first piece of the jigsaw – a parcel of desert land, on the Giza Plateau above the River Nile, with views of the Pyramids of Cheops and Chephren and the rooftops of Cairo – she collected antiques from France and around the world for the future home, which, almost miraculously, would fit the finished space perfectly.

Above all else Dar al Mansour is a love letter to my mother. She adored houses and interior decoration and always knew I had a dream, which she shared, to build a house that would dazzle and echo her love and appreciation of beautiful things. Sadly, she did not live long enough to see the scale and magnificence of this house. She had introduced into our lives and homes elements of Parisian chic alongside Middle Eastern mystique, always with an artist's observant eye for detail. Chinese vases of ancient dynasties as well as Aubusson carpets and Sèvres porcelain.

Over the course of more than a decade, I gradually purchased the other parcels of land that I needed. It was at a very early stage in the project, and well before the plans for the house were finalised, that I engaged one of the foremost landscape architects of the twentieth century, Sir Geoffrey Jellicoe. I wanted water to be a key component of the development, and Sir Geoffrey, by then in his nineties, had for decades been world-renowned for his water features, including his signature characteristics of canals, weirs and bridges. One of his most famous commissions was an acre of land in Surrey, England, to honour John F. Kennedy. The JFK Memorial Landscape, which Sir Geoffrey designed in 1964, the year after the president's assassination, was jointly dedicated in 1965 by Queen Elizabeth II and the president's widow, Jackie Kennedy.

To honour Egypt, his design for Dar al Mansour devised a series of platforms and layered gardens that would evoke the path of Africa's longest river, from Lake Victoria through the Delta to the Mediterranean. We discussed having the sound of water play everywhere you go in the gardens as you come across the elegant fountains and Greek- and Roman-style statues. His concept featured three focal points: the 'Garden of Contemplation' to the east of the site; the 'Gardens for the Many' to the west; and the 'Underworld', where water would gush down a chute to the level below. As work progressed, we took the project to the French landscape designer Eric Vachetto, who interpreted Sir Geoffrey's ideas and selected species that would thrive in Cairo's climate. One of my favourite corners is the ornate tea pavilion at the edge of the garden, close to the main pool, from where I like to sit and look across Cairo and beyond.

Thousands worked on the project – landscape architects and artisans, carpet layers and carpenters, plasterers and plumbers. The Cairo population was exploding, and to ensure our home would not be swamped or overlooked by future development, we did what initially seemed impossible by attaining permissions to raise the land by about 14 metres, a man-made mound roughly equivalent in height to a four-storey property.

For the house, originally, I envisioned that it would be wholly Islamic, but over time this vision shifted. Ultimately, I sought a design that would both reflect architectural history while embracing modernity, that would have a connection to the classical era and yet be undeniably a part of the Muslim world. We took proposals from several architects, but none managed an equal marriage of European, Egyptian and Ottoman influences that I wanted. Rawya, who studied fine art at Sotheby's and Christie's in London, was an experienced interior designer and decorator, agreed to take over the project. This made complete sense in terms of her ability to interpret the way I wanted to live and how I wanted to express my feelings about entertaining, family life and style.

Finalising the designs took five years and it took a further three years to obtain the necessary permits. Rawya moved on-site in 2007, managing 20 different architects and 250 contractors. Every possible event or comfort was considered, each member of the family catered for – from the contemporary-designed private suites for Loutfy and Mansour on the first floor to the living quarters for Fafy and me on the second floor. Below ground, there is a stylish dance and party space with a kitchen that is capable of catering for up to 200 people. By the time it was completed, it was Rawya's largest project and the whole family considered it to be a great achievement.

The exterior of the property features striped masonry called *ablaq*, an Islamic technique, that uses alternate rows of light and dark stones or bricks. Inside the three-storey building are interior fountains, generous windows and Romanesque arches and columns. Many of the features both inside and out, including the iron gates, are painted a vivid blue, one of my favourite colours. The defining feature of the home is a 12-metre-high dome that illuminates the marbled entrance hall below; it was inspired by a similar dome at the Old Cataract Hotel. In the separate poolhouse, Byzantine-style lanterns hang from the ceilings of the walkway around the edge of the building, while the stone-and-gesso ceiling inside the poolhouse was inspired by the Royal

Pavilion in Brighton, England, the seafront retreat built in the late-eighteenth century for the future King George IV.

This is a house which is part theatre and part art exhibition. It is a display of Art Deco furniture and lines from Ralph Lauren and Andrew Martin. It is a showcase and treat for all the senses, thanks to Rawya and her desire to explore history and modernity, technology and tradition to make a home that is memorable and meaningful to all the family. I want to thank my beloved sister for her commitment and dedication to this project and for creating something extraordinary.

Homes, I believe, reflect our lives: they are an extension of our imagination, hopes, fears and taste. They are far more than mere bricks and mortar, or even marble and stone. They represent who we are and to what we aspire.

Walt Disney understood this with his trademark of a fantasy castle with Romanesque turrets and towers that he created as the company logo, based on the fantastical castle of King Ludwig of Bavaria. For Disney it was about sparking our imagination to make us feel dreams can come true.

Margaret Thatcher grasped the transformative potential of property by creating a new home-owning democracy in the UK in the 1980s, selling state-owned homes to council tenants to allow them to take control of their lives. She equated property with ownership and aspiration, and this defined Thatcher's turbo-charged form of capitalism.

The desire to build and provide homes has become a defining trope of our family over the last ten years. Our aim as a family has been to widen our remit and to make as large an impact on Egypt through housing. While Dar al Mansour is a very private place that we only open for charity events and entertaining, what we are now doing in the west of Cairo dwarves it in scale and ambition. Thanks to Yasseen's singular ambition and vision, we are building a city.

No family in Egypt has ever tried such an ambitious building project. The city of Badya, once completed, will provide homes for more than 270,000 people. It is literally carving a new metropolis for people in Cairo to inhabit. In terms of scale, it will be one-third the size of Manhattan, while it will house more people than the British towns of Reading and Guildford combined. We will invest capital to redefine how people live in the capital.

Much of the country's residential space traditionally has been squeezed into a narrow strip of fertile land that surrounds the Nile. However, new cities are being created amid a construction boom that the government hopes will eventually increase the proportion of the country's land utilised for housing from 7% to 14%.

At Badya we are thinking far beyond just houses. We are building a new university within the city, which, we believe, will be the greenest academic university on the planet. There will be wind corridors and the latest in water technology for reusing and recycling this precious commodity. Most residents will be just a two-minute stroll away from green areas filled with botanical life and water elements. Neighbourhoods will be interweaved with pathways to promote walking and cycling in safe, breathable atmospheres. Central plazas promoting less motorised transport will highlight the centre of each residential block and will be interlocked with scenic bike lanes and footpaths to the many others throughout the splendour of Badya. Every destination can be reached easily by public transport, car or bike. We believe it will be the first city in the Middle East and North Africa to be in full compliance with the UN's sustainable development goals.

This is a city carved out of desert and this book is being printed just as the foundations are placed in the rock in the base of the desert. Cairo is vast and in need of new housing. This injection of money from the private sector and government backing will generate not just Egypt's first twenty-first-century city, but also a place where over a million jobs will be provided. I am reminded of the American Dream of the 1950s where houses were built in gracious spaces and the aspirations of the generation for living a more self-sufficient life propelled the work ethic and inspired a different way to live.

I must pay tribute to my brother Yasseen who has been the driving force behind this building bonanza. I don't wish to steal his thunder, but as Palm Hills' second largest shareholder, I could not be prouder to be associated with this project. This is a legacy that we want to share with Cairo, a gift from the Mansour family to Egypt, which will always have a place in our heart.

If I expressed at the start of this chapter some scepticism about whether the home is where the heart is, maybe I was a little impulsive. It certainly can be precisely that. I am banking on that being the case with Dar al Mansour and Badya. Brick by brick, step by step, we have moved forward, relying on ambition and aspiration to motivate us in business and now, more the ever, in building a city. We have always gained inspiration and strength from Egypt as the greatest creator of architectural wonder and have been motivated by that. We hope we can make one small step with the Mansour Group, amid those giant steps for mankind.

CHAPTER THIRTEEN

'We shall not cease from exploration'

Time marches fast and the Old Testament is plain and stark on the span of a man's life: 'Three score and ten'. Well, I have passed that 70 marker and am not ready to put on the brakes. Even if retirement meant lounging around all day on the deck of a yacht in the Mediterranean that would, at best, send me to sleep, or, at worst, mad with boredom! I am too restless. My brain whirrs constantly trying to find ways to do things better or differently and my curiosity remains undimmed. I live to move forwards. Never more so than today as 300,000 people have their livelihoods tied to our companies and my ambition remains for them to prosper and for our companies to grow.

As one of the largest private companies in the Middle East, I sometimes think back to my first faltering steps in business all those years ago in Alabama when I was in my early twenties. Then

I combined the inexperience of youth with what I had learned from my MBA and what I had gleaned from watching and listening to my father at work. It took time to feel confident as I tried to offer advice as a fixer-consultant to local firms. The essential ingredient in my modus operandi, more than anything else, was a hunger to prosper. Before relocating to Alabama I had struggled financially as an undergraduate in North Carolina, and was determined to never live like that again.

For me fortitude has proved to be the most formidable foe against any and every adversary. I learned that the hard way. It was a combination of chutzpah and common sense, always flying by the seat of my pants as, although I had studied cash flow and planning systems during my MBA, it was actually doing the work rather than dreaming or planning it that was to take me to a profitable path for myself and, thankfully, also for our clients.

During this time, my father was fighting to re-establish his cotton business after all his assets had been stripped and so, inevitably, Egypt was always at the forefront of my mind. It was both sweet and sour; a giver and a taker of assets and opportunities; it brought great fortune and also left us with nothing. Like a farmer with a new spring crop in a difficult climate, all we could do was continue planting new seeds. Quickly, I came to realise that you have to think, however pressing your short-term needs are. We took risks and gave our all to make our ideas work. Our eventual two main business pillars – the automobile sector and Caterpillar opportunity – prospered beyond our wildest dreams. The returns we have generated on modest investments in those businesses have been extraordinary. Egypt is, and always was, at the centre of what I do and who I am, alongside an absolute belief in the benefits of hard work.

Egypt is my genesis and from where our company grew into a global empire. Although my base is now in London, we are defined by Egypt. It was important to become global but the beating heart of our empire started on home soil in my father's country of birth, where I had ridden horses across the sands hills and desert landscapes in the shadow of the Pyramids. I carry Egypt in my blood and heart but am also a citizen of the world whose home in London makes me feel grateful and is a place to which I can also say I belong.

What I own and run today stretches from Cairo to California. It started from watching my father work without pause in Alexandria. He never stopped. Reputation was everything. His word was his bond and that defined and moulded his success. He was very proud of our family history as well as our country's heritage. He showed me great monuments from Giza to Luxor. He was patriotic to his core and, of course, Egyptian cotton was a defining part of him as well as his signature – making and exporting the finest quality cloth all over the world.

The iconic identity of Egypt for most people is defined by the Pyramids, which were what I saw with wondrous eyes growing up. They are also the pinnacle of what an extreme vision and enormous hard work, thought up by the pharaohs and the people who built them, can result in. That incredible wonder still stirs something majestic in me, which has never left me, and never will. They may well be just blocks of stone, but it is layer upon layer of history, a permanent remembrance of family, fortune and fable. It inspired me and continues to be inspiring to many others. Those proud silhouettes are seared into my mind as a tribute to family and fortune, to past and future, that honours the dead and feeds the imagination of the living. They represent both hope and glory.

Growing up in Egypt I was always happiest when playing with Dinky model cars in the sand. I could identify the latest American automobiles as they zoomed along Alexandria's Corniche – one of my earliest memories is my father pointing to different cars and saying, 'What kind of car is that?' and I would say, 'It's an Oldsmobile ... Studebaker ... Pontiac ... Cadillac ... Mercedes ..' I loved games of table football with my brothers and was always mesmerised by football in the street played by boys in bare feet. I did not know then how dreams and fortunes can be made by holding on to what we like doing, to those early inspirations and dreams. Cars and football. Family and friends. Making and marketing. Motivating and manufacturing. Merging and acquiring. Learning, listening, leading. Egypt has a way of casting a spell and enabling me to do things. When my father asked me to return from America in 1973, I was initially reluctant. But I was so glad that I could return with American optimism and a can-do attitude. It was daunting as we had a political system back then that did not immediately favour private entrepreneurs. It was a land of brilliant opportunities but with great poverty and challenges. I was always aware of huge divides but knew the best way to heal such divisions and difficulties was through economic growth. Generating employment and creating opportunities have defined so much of the path I have taken.

As a boy I was taken to those ancient Pyramids of Giza, those iconic stone symbols of genius and power. A true wonder of the world, and it was on my doorstep. The Pyramids are a symbol of hope. Impossible things that were built. What did Egyptians do all those millennia back? They made an impact. They built lasting structures. They created legacy. Egypt was my beginning and will continue to define me until the very end.

Egypt created possibly the highest civilisation ever forged. Our regal historic past is potent: pharaohs, Cleopatra, sarcophagi and jewels unmatched in terms of aesthetic glamour, a heritage that catches the imagination of the world. Many of the artefacts and narrative of several millennia today are displayed afresh in the Grand Egyptian Museum, the largest and, surely, the greatest museum of ancient times in the world. I say this with particular pride as I play a small part in this monumental museum as one of the only trustees on its board from the private sector. The museum was awaiting its official opening as I wrote this book and is destined to be one of the most popular museums on the planet.

I see Egypt as a place defined by its historic uniqueness and, also, as a place for building dreams and taking opportunities: like the ebb and flow of the Nile, my family's life has seen great lows and highs, from creation to destruction and back again. In the more recent past we have seen that on an epic scale with Covid-19 impacting the two countries I love most. Both, fortunately, survived great difficulties during the pandemic, and while masks and curfews, laws and regulations left us in our homes and caused pain, grief and mourning for so many thousands, it did see an end to some opportunities but also provided new technical innovations like Zoom. Our way of working was upended and we experienced grief as well as economic loss. The pandemic, as with all crises, brought reflection and reactions.

Covid-19 concentrated the entire world's mind. We learned how to inspire, survive and prosper when the world was in danger of grinding to a halt. Sitting in my house in London on my own, masks and gloves at the front door, fears accelerating, travel suspended, all these restrictions and rules left a permanent scar on the country. In the UK alone more than 200,000 died. However, our companies have stood strong and have survived. But it was a period to test your character and values. To decide what you protect and how you value all you do and want. My family and I knew we had to give. We have been so fortunate and have always gained strength from giving just as we gained opportunities when people gave to us in our early days. Second chances are a theme of my life. I was given one at university. My father was even given a third chance to build a business after twice having it taken from him. Hence why the resurrection and restoration of the museum in Cairo symbolises so much to me.

I have learned that passion and purpose are vital ingredients in building a legacy. Small strategic steps are exactly what we did with the Lead Foundation, our not-for-profit. Often, I saw how these women had ambitions to do what I did in my twenties, to take steps to be financially independent, to prosper as a small business, always to reach forward and to have ambitious hopes and dreams. Nothing has made me prouder in my career than witnessing the success and growth of the Lead Foundation.

We had to support countries during the pandemic. When Covid-19 hit Egypt, my brothers and I gave $11.5 million to support the fight against the virus and fund the purchase of personal protective equipment (PPE), ambulances and medical supplies. We hoped to encourage other businesspeople in Egypt to follow suit. We made donations to help fight the pandemic in African countries, including Nigeria and Uganda. Our view is that we have to make a difference to the areas we serve. As a family company, in times of difficulty, you make sure that you look after your people and do all that you can to support your communities. The private sector has got a role to play in supporting governments and looking after their people in these critical times. I think family businesses have a particular duty to help in such emergencies.

I was also moved to give in the UK as I saw the strangulation on the economy as the country closed down and struggled to reopen. I love Britain: its people, way of life, strong safe-guarding legal system, landscapes and cities. I love its traditions and sense of humour and the candour and straight-dealing of the people. The UK has given me a second home and security, as well as a sanctuary and base to foster a global business. And it has given me a third chance in my life. This is why it fills me with such pride to be able to do whatever I can to serve the country. I was so honoured to be appointed as senior treasurer of the UK Conservative

Party in December 2022. The party of Churchill is a great political movement and one of the oldest political parties in the world and it gives me enormous pride to serve.

Another moment of clarity was when I was approached to contribute to a national memorial at St Paul's Cathedral in London for the people who had died due to Covid-19 complications in the UK. I am instinctive in making decisions and I felt an immediate desire to help mark this historic pandemic, and I liked the way that this was a digital memorial as well as the first new stone structure to be added to the great cathedral since Christopher Wren laid its foundation stones in the seventeenth century.

Two epic monuments in two great countries: the Pyramids and St Paul's. They are emblematic of their different countries and are glorious icons known across the globe. They trigger patriotic faith and belief, and are able to take death while elevating us all to a higher plain of thought, philosophy and prayer. I was so proud to be able to contribute to the St Paul's memorial. It linked to my gratitude to Britain and marked my shared grief over the losses that had left Britain mourning on a scale not seen since World War II. It was a coalition of people of different faiths – Muslims, Jews, Christians and atheists – that touched the soul in combination with the overwhelming need for people to put other people first.

I returned to my memory as a boy of seeing the Pyramids when I took my family to see the memorial at St Paul's. They wondered at the dome and the echoing sounds of the Whispering Gallery. The cathedral is one of the most famous and recognisable sights in London. Its dome, framed by the spires of Wren's architectural design, has dominated the city skyline for over three centuries and has borne witness to the funerals of Lord Nelson and Winston Churchill; the jubilee celebrations of Queen Victoria; and the wedding of Charles and Diana.

The cathedral was a project that took leadership and needed vision, as well as money, to succeed and prosper. In our own ways, we are all Christopher Wrens; trying to build and make something worthwhile. They wanted things to last. They wanted to celebrate what people can do when they come together. They stood together. They had vision and were lucky enough to be able to fulfil it.

• • •

So, how do I sum everything up? Luck should be acknowledged once more. I am one of the luckiest people on the planet, having overcome huge medical challenges before being able to achieve wealth and construct a business empire that is global and still expanding. The value in my life is also fundamentally measured in having a family who mean everything to me.

Hard work, and an insatiable, never quenched thirst to succeed, grow and create opportunities for my family and others are so important too. None of what I have has been achieved without great effort. Hard work is the defining quality that I have espoused over my years in business. I learned, too, what a good time without hard endeavour brings: a butterfly existence with no investment of time and effort, which means little chance to grow and prosper. I experienced a certain degree of happy idleness as a footloose and carefree student in my first months in the US, but at NC State and Amedeo's, and so many other times and places later, I learned that nothing prospers without putting in the work.

I have always taken a values-driven approach. Integrity, honesty and transparency are the roots that underpin our empire. Our logo shows two hands: cradling and nurturing. I can recall a meeting with a company founder who sat at the head of the table with his portrait hanging on the wall behind him. That is not my style, and I don't think it is the Egyptian culture. I like to think I project authority in a more understated way. I can certainly get tough when it is warranted but I do not care for such overt displays of power and authority. I aim to lead by example, and I like to think that the loyalty of so many people who have worked for me is a measure that this approach has been effective.

You must be open and honest, which can lead to making tough choices or saying things that people do not want to hear. The layoffs we had to make to keep our automotive business afloat during the 1980s were devastating for those concerned, and letting people know was very painful for us. You need to be upfront and communicate through both the hard and good times.

Perseverance is also key. It is not because we were lucky and struck oil that we were able to be so fortunate and have more than I ever dreamed of as a young man. It's been a hard slog: it's been never giving up. Always being honest with your values. Caring for people. Fighting for what is right. Having a vision. Knowing what really matters in life. If I had to summarise what was needed, it would be a desire to win, or even a necessity to win.

I have a relatively simple philosophy which is that there is no gain without some pain. You must sacrifice something in your life to achieve. Work never was a 9–5 job for me. Every day in the morning I wake up looking forward to going to work because I love what I do. I love creating, building things and am inspired by being ahead of the curve by being one of the first Egyptian families to expand globally and, later, establish a family office. Backing women entrepreneurs through the Lead Foundation was groundbreaking in Egypt. Building a Major League Soccer organisation in San Diego, California from scratch is another case in point.

I never was a kid who crammed or studied very hard, but I changed as I saw the bigger picture. A seismic moment was when my father passed away; that devastating experience transformed me. Yes, I was surrounded by my mother and siblings, and they were an enormous comfort and support for me during that terrible time. But I knew then that there was no one to fall back on. My father had been my rock, and it was now up to me. My ambition hardened and I knew I needed to focus on making what we did successful.

Within a few years I started my own family and my sons soon became my priority. The next generation stirred me to want to make our family business even more successful than it had been by the time of their births. I wanted to fulfil my father's dreams, which in turn became the dreams of my sons. I hope one day that these dreams will be shared by my grandchildren as I have dedicated my working life to preserving the honour and dignity of the Mansour name, which is why our personal conduct is so important. The way the business operates reflects on our name, and the way we conduct ourselves reflects on the company. The link is inextricable.

The business-building part is a drive and a passion that is never-ending. Endless curiosity drives more ideas, more innovation. When Michael Jordan, Mo Salah or Roger Federer win a championship, they are constantly striving to improve. For me, success was never about the money. It is about the sense of achievement and accomplishment. When we founded the automotive business, we thought selling 100 cars a year would be a success. When we reached 1,000, then 10,000, we did not rest on our laurels. We now sell around 100,000 each year and I have ambitions to hit a higher sum. We have returned 17,000 times our capital in the automotive business and 20,000 times our capital in the Caterpillar business. Those exceptional numbers make me so proud, because to achieve something like that once is an amazing feat, but to do so twice feels like a miracle to me. I am enormously grateful to everyone who has dedicated so much of their working lives to take us to these great heights.

I've always set myself goals and thrive on that challenge. When I owed $454 to my fraternity and got a job waiting tables, I knew it would take several months to pay it back. It was a lot of money at the time, and my tips were usually less than a dollar. But I had a goal to aim for, and I knew I would have to work relentlessly hard, over long hours, to achieve that goal; it did not deter me, it inspired me. Ever since then, I have thrived on setting myself new goals and trying to achieve them in the most honourable way.

When I reach the summit, I look for the next mountain to climb. I consider myself a risk-taker. Walking again, or defeating cancer as a young man, did not make me think I was invincible – they made me realise what was at stake and the very fragility of my existence. However, overcoming those hardships gave me a sense of purpose and I did not want to squander an opportunity. I was not reckless but did take calculated risks, including the Unatrac acquisition, accepting a position in the government, and launching Man Capital. Maybe if you start from zero, as I did, you have nothing to lose. The thirst I had as 'Mo' while waiting on tables has never been fully quenched. I thirst for more.

Life has not been easy for me. It has been a road of many challenges, myriad obstacles that I have had to find different ways to overcome, which shaped my character and personality. When I was a younger man, people told me I could be difficult to live with, be with or work with. It was my way or the highway. But like everyone you adjust over time and your experience, your priorities mature and you then begin to realise what is important.

What is my legacy? I very much hope that my great-grandchildren will one day consider what my siblings and I achieved and think this is how to live a life: learn lessons from the ups and downs of a long life, plant acorns so as to guarantee a future by seeing them transform from saplings into strong, mighty oaks.

Writing this book has been a tonic, rich and joyous while sometimes painful and cathartic. How to humbly sum up the meaning of a life? I recently came across, through a friend of mine, one of the shortest poems ever written and it amused me, not least due to my love of tea, but because it made me think. It is an elegant seven-word poem written by Samuel Menashe, a New Yorker, who also fell in love with Britain and was first published in the UK.

The poem simply says:

A pot poured out
Fulfils its spout

It must be one of the shortest poems ever written but it shines like a tiny diamond looking up from the silt. I like it because it is practical, simple and humble, yet clever. Even though it is not as grand or totemic in its stature as, say, St Paul's or the Pyramids, it is a simple call for everything in life to be purposeful and have some meaning. It takes the simplest image of something that a great majority of us use every day, and it unearths a beauty, a perfection and aspiration of what we should do in life. Even the smallest things in our lifetime can mirror the greatest ambitions and achievements. I think of it as a farewell sign of what we must all do: to do all we can, to give all we can, to work as hard as we can and to take opportunities at every turn and use them. They are often God-given but man-made.

I have been so lucky and have loved building this life. It is my privilege to share some of it with you in this book.

'If at first you don't succeed, try, try and try again.'

Attributed to Robert the Bruce, King of Scotland (1274–1329)

Acknowledgements

I am so grateful for the support of my family, especially my wife Fafy, sons Mansour and Loutfy, brothers Youssef and Yasseen and sister Rawya my nephews, nieces and cousins, who I love dearly. The memory of my father and mother inspired these memoirs, and always my beloved late brother Ismail is in my heart.

In terms of the production of this book, special thanks are due to my co-writer Andrew Cave, my communications director Dominic Tonner, and Elizabeth Bond at Penguin Random House.

Finally, I want to pay a special tribute to all past and present employees of the Mansour Group. Everything we have achieved is down to you.

Index

MM indicates Mohamed Mansour.